"If you love your pastor, read this book, and then put it into practice. And if you are looking for a pastor, before you do anything else, make sure everyone on the search committee reads *How to Keep the Pastor You Love*. It is a gift that will strengthen the body of Christ."

DR. RAY PRITCHARD, SENIOR PASTOR,
CALVARY MEMORIAL CHURCH, AND AUTHOR OF
AN ANCHOR FOR THE SOUL

"For many years, we have seen an appropriate emphasis on church growth, but more recently attention has been given to church health. The well-being of the church and its leadership is an integral part of church health, and Jane Rubietta, writing from the perspective of a pastor's wife, has valuable insight to share."

JILL BRISCOE, AUTHOR, SPEAKER AND EDITOR OF *JUST BETWEEN US*,
A MAGAZINE FOR MINISTRY WIVES

"For those of us who work with pastors, the evidence of crisis in the ministry hits us between the eyes. Jane Rubietta has contributed wise and practical helps for those lay leaders who are concerned about keeping the pastor they love. We wish we could put this book in the hands of every elder group, every session, every governing council as emergency intervention."

DAVID AND KAREN MAINS, CODIRECTORS OF MAINSTAY

"A valuable tool to place in the hands of concerned church members and church officials, every pastor of every local church and each clergy spouse. I find the faithfulness of the author shining brightly all through the work."

REV. CHARLES CHAKOUR, PASTOR AND AUTHOR
OF *BUILDING CLERGY COMPENSATION*

How to
KEEP THE PASTOR YOU LOVE

Jane Rubietta

InterVarsity Press
Downers Grove, Illinois

InterVarsity Press
P.O. Box 1400, Downers Grove, IL 60515-1426
World Wide Web: www.ivpress.com
E-mail: mail@ivpress.com

InterVarsity Press® is the book-publishing division of InterVarsity Christian Fellowship/USA®, a student movement active on campus at hundreds of universities, colleges and schools of nursing in the United States of America, and a member movement of the International Fellowship of Evangelical Students. For information about local and regional activities, write Public Relations Dept., InterVarsity Christian Fellowship/USA, 6400 Schroeder Rd., P.O. Box 7895, Madison, WI 53707-7895, or visit the IVCF website at <www.ivcf.org>.

All Scripture quotations, unless otherwise indicated, are taken from the Holy Bible, New International Version®. NIV®. *Copyright ©1973, 1978, 1984 by International Bible Society. Used by permission of Zondervan Publishing House. All rights reserved.*

Financial information is provided with the understanding that it does not constitute tax, legal, accounting or other professional service.

Cover photograph: R. Creation/Photonica

The poem "Moving Day," written by Kathy Leithner, is used by permission.

ISBN 0-8308-2319-0

Printed in the United States of America ∞

Library of Congress Cataloging-in-Publication Data

Rubietta, Jane.
    How to keep the pastor you love/Jane Rubietta.
     p. cm.
    Includes bibliographical references.
    ISBN 0-8308-2319-0 (pbk.: alk. paper)
    1. Clergy—Office. 2. Interpersonal relations—Religious aspects—Christianity. 3. Church etiquette. I. Title.
BV660.3 .R83 2002
253'.2—dc21   2002017259

| P | 17 | 16 | 15 | 14 | 13 | 12 | 11 | 10 | 9 | 8 | 7 | 6 | 5 | 4 | 3 | 2 | 1 |
| Y | 15 | 14 | 13 | 12 | 11 | 10 | 09 | 08 | 07 | 06 | 05 | 04 | 03 | 02 | | | |

Dedicated
to clergy and their families throughout the ages,
who have heard and heeded God's call to service,
often at great cost to themselves: you have never lost sight of the privilege
and miracle of being God's spokespeople

CONTENTS

Acknowledgments

A tremendous, bottom-of-my-heart-and-soul thank you to . . .

The people in ministry who shaped me while I observed and benefited from their Christlike leadership and servanthood: from churches of childhood to the churches where my husband has served, including Park Avenue Church in Minneapolis, Minnesota; Florence Station, Morris, Joliet and Grayslake, Illinois; and the people in those churches who accepted and loved us, who forgave us our many failings and encouraged us to live out God's call on our lives.

Ray and Norma Allison, and Bill and Sally Irwin: your care for our children helped them bloom and helped us continue in ministry.

Rev. Phil and Lois Whisenhunt: most significant role models for ministry and marriage, exemplifying the grace and love of our Lord Jesus with an unending enthusiasm, and claiming me as one of your own children.

Bishop C. Joseph Sprague, Bishop Jonathan Keaton and Rev. Duk Kwon: all of you believed in and supported God's leading in my life; Rev. Charles Chakour, former treasurer of the United Methodist Church, Northern Illinois Conference, my mentor in clergy finances for fifteen years, and Lonnie Chafin, his successor.

My covenant group for nearly a decade—Adele Calhoun, Karen Mains, Linda Richardson, Marilyn Stewart and Sibyl Towner: for holding me on the journey of integrity as a woman in professional ministry as well as a woman, wife, mother, friend. Your part in the transformation process both humbles and shapes me. You have created a pietà for me, and I am deeply grateful for your presence in my life.

My writers' group of ten years—Lynn Austin, Joy Bocanegra and Cleo Lampos: for keeping me in the road and calling me to accountability (with such love and compassion and laughter and corn chips) for the gifts and calling God has given me.

Four women from those early years in ministry who patched me together and held me in place 'til the glue dried—Marge Olson, Pat Hunter, Sue Mavek and Andrea Schmitke: for unearthing the embers of gifts and starting the fanning process;

The people at the Grayslake Library (and before them the people in Joliet, Illinois), who searched out every obscure jot and tittle possible with good humor and interest; Ian Evison at the Alban Institute and Eldon Fry, chaplain at Focus on the Family, for invaluable research support.

The countless clergy, spouses and children who shared via interviews and informal surveys their greatest joys and sorrows in ministry: your names and some details have been changed but your love and calling remain clear.

Cindy Bunch at InterVarsity Press and all the passionate people there who equip the saints for works of service: thank you for believing in the premise of *How to Keep the Pastor You Love* and for desiring to support people in ministry.

My parents, Jack and Shirley Henderson, who always have a book going, and who taught me to love words from infancy: there is no doubt that the love of a well-written book taught me to love the Word and the Author of the Word.

My parents by marriage, Jim and Marie Rubietta, without whose love and help we could not juggle our callings and our family life: you have taught me much about acceptance and forgiveness.

My children, Zak, Ruthie, Josh: you keep reminding me to pay attention, to notice what God is doing and to laugh; seeing God at work in your hearts is all I could ever want. Thank you for loving me even when I am scatterbrained or task-oriented.

My husband, Rich, whose love, laughter and faith continue to inspire me: you believed in God's work in me when I didn't believe in myself, and that faith opened doors for Christ to push me through: thank you for not giving up on me.

And to my gracious God and Savior: for showing me mercy when I deserve judgement; for giving me life in the face of death; for doing "immeasurably more than all we can ask or imagine, . . . to him be glory in the church and in Christ Jesus throughout all generations."

Introduction

"What if you could change the world by doing just one thing?" I asked a group of elders, deacons and heads of pastor-parish committees. "In only a few minutes a day, or even a week—would you do it?"

They looked at me with disbelief; a few nodded their heads warily.

"Pray for your pastor."

The people still looked at me, though with greater disbelief. I went on, "If you were to regularly pray for your pastors, to invite God's presence and power into their ministries and their homes, they would be energized and directed in the work God has for them. God's work would be done in the church and in society, because you're taking care of your pastor. The world would be changed because of those prayers."

This is not isolated, new millennium thinking. Paul said long ago, "But we request of you . . . that you appreciate those who diligently labor among you, and have charge over you in the Lord and give you instruction, and that you esteem them very highly in love because of their work" (1 Thess 5:12-13 NASB).

God's desire is that we honor our clergy, that their hearts

might be refreshed in Christ for the work of the kingdom (Philem 20). If you don't feel like you really love your pastor or even know your pastor, try these pages on for size. The correlation between stunted church growth and pastoral turnover is alarming. Caring for those in ministry can stem the wholesale change of staff happening in many local churches.

How to Keep the Pastor You Love is win-win. You, the pastor's family, the church, the community and God win when the pastor is honored, loved and encouraged. For people in ministry, the partly-dones and the not-dones far outnumber the well-dones and leave pastors too often undone. Everyone, including ministers, needs to hear "Well done" a few times on earth to sweeten the journey to heaven when our God says, "Well done, good and faithful servant. Enter into the joy of your master."

Maximizing This Resource

Individuals, couples, families, church boards or committees, small groups, Sunday school classes—anyone can use and apply *How to Keep the Pastor You Love*. District superintendents, supervising pastors and church conferences likewise can use this resource in training leadership and in supporting the pastors to whom they minister. Principles within for prayer, building up, communication and support are applicable to any reader and to the reader's role and responsibility in the local church. Each chapter contains places of application, Scriptures for a solid foundation of care, and a call to prayer. From moving in to moving out, from communication to conflict, from family to finance, from parsonage to pain, the topics in this book connect instantly to any local church.

Ministers, too, benefit from working through *How to Keep the Pastor You Love*. People in ministry serve, not because they will be rewarded with kudos and hugs and hot apple pie (al-

though these items sure do encourage!) but because God has
called them into service. "For the Pastor" sections throughout
each chapter keep ministers asking themselves the hard questions, preventing "poor me" thinking. These become a basis for
accountability before God, with spouses if married and in small
groups of others in ministry. Using *How to Keep the Pastor You
Love* in clergy clusters, ministerial support groups or accountability groups is ideal. Tough issues and to-the-point questions
ask those in ministry to be honest, vulnerable and to walk a
straight line of integrity in ministry, creating companionship on
an often lonely journey.

Real Change

For true change to happen in our churches, caring for those in
ministry, whether associate or youth pastors or the solo or
senior pastor, must increase. For obvious reasons this type of
care cannot be initiated by the clergy. What's recommended is
establishing a committee, task force or designated liaison
responsible for seeing that pastor care is intentional, systematic
and regularly evaluated.

When beginning to care for your clergy, it is important to
consider personality types, needs and relational style, and to
find a balance between uninvolvement and incessant interaction. When in doubt, asking is always appropriate.

As we become the body of Christ to our ministers, they will
be better equipped to "run with perseverance the race" that is
marked out for them (Heb 12:1). And God will honor our
faithfulness and obedience as we "share all good things" with
the one who teaches (Gal 6:6), that the blessing of God might
rest on our households (Ezek 44:28-30).

Further resources are available at the InterVarsity Press website <www.ivpress.com>.

1

A New Definition for "Pastoral Care"

And now, friends, we ask you to honor those leaders
who work so hard for you,
who have been given the responsibility of
urging and guiding you along in your obedience.
Overwhelm them with appreciation and love!

1 THESSALONIANS 5:12-13
(THE MESSAGE)

I squinted against the early morning brightness. My eyelids scraped like sandpaper against my eyes. Having visited relatives on the East Coast, my husband Rich and I drove through the night with our three children for the last hurrah of our vacation—a few days with my family in the Midwest. Close to their house, I noticed a familiar car following. We pulled into the driveway, the other car roaring in behind.

My brother John jumped out, his tired face matching the way I felt. He came around to my side of the car. My heart sank. With the sun hovering at the tree line, he should have been inside enjoying his first jolt of morning coffee. The break in routine seemed ominous.

"Nice timing." I tried to smile around my fear.

"Grandmom died about ten minutes ago, Jane." He clenched his hands at his sides. "Mom's there now. Do you want to come?"

Numbness settled over my soul. My dry eyes refused to shed tears as John pulled me to him in a hug. I moved through the next three days in a frozen state.

The day after the funeral my husband, a pastor, was expected in the pulpit in Illinois. There was no time to grieve and remember and laugh with relatives after the service. We reloaded our car and made the journey back to our own home, heavy-hearted, quiet and lonely. A carefree getaway full of family memories closed on a grief-filled note.

Back in church, Rich asked for prayers as we coped with our loss. This was not the place I wanted to begin feeling the pain, so I sat stiffly in the pew, palms sweating. Chills chased over my body.

The postlude sounded. People collected bags, babies, bulletins. I lingered in the foyer, hesitant to approach anyone as grief nibbled at my composure. No one offered sympathy, hugged me or simply said, "I'm sorry." After ten miserable minutes, I gathered the children and bolted for home. Our vacation concluded with a loved one's funeral, but the anguish and isolation had just begun.

"Did anyone say anything to you after the service, Jane?" my husband asked. When I shook my head, multiple expressions flashed across his face: surprise, anger and sadness.

As a pastoral family, we faced a surprising turnabout. Whereas our role in others' grief was to comfort, there seemed to be no clear guidelines for the congregation's response in the reverse situation when we needed care. Who ministers to the minister's family?

A New Look at Pastoral Care: Overwhelmed but Not with Love

Ours is not the only family to fall through the void. Much research, reading and interviewing yield a sobering conclusion. According to H. B. London, head of the pastoral ministries department at Focus on the Family, "Four words characterize how many ministers feel. They are: isolation, loneliness, insecurity, and inadequacy."[1]

Historically, pastoral care has not meant instruction in caring for one's pastor. It has always meant a pastor's care for the congregation. Clergy are professional burden bearers in many ways. Unfortunately, the application of "bear one another's burdens" (Gal 6:2) often stops somewhere short of bearing the burdens for the minister and family. However, Scripture portrays clearly the supporting roles the people of God are to play in the lives of those in ministry. "Honor those leaders who work so hard for you," 1 Thessalonians 5:12-13 reads, to "overwhelm them with appreciation and love!" (The Message).

Don, a pastor in a mainline denomination, remembered getting a card a day for an entire month as the church celebrated their clergy. "It was very affirming," he said. "What would it be like to be affirmed throughout the whole year?" The congregation, organized initially by Don's secretary, did not realize the tremendous effect such affirmation had on their hard-working minister. But because the desire to care for the pastor initiated with church personnel, the congregation did not continue the effort. Perhaps a lack of supporting evidence as to why the clergy need and deserve such affirmation contributed to the one-time attempt.

Quittin' Time?

An atmosphere of love, acceptance and affirmation makes staying in the church appealing, even in the face of conflict. Their absence adds impetus to thoughts of quitting. In the book *Seven Promises of a Promise Keeper,* contributing author Dale Schafler says, "Eighty percent of all pastors responding had thought about quitting in the last three months."[2]

Mark, pastoring his current church for eight years, said, "I think about quitting twice a week." Marion, a pastor in New Hampshire, admitted, "Sure I think about leaving the ministry. Anyone who says they do not consider quitting, even fleetingly, is lying."

FOR THE PASTOR
1. When was the last time you thought about quitting?
2. What precipitated that feeling? Exhaustion? Spiritual depletion?
   Conflict with a parishioner? Family problems?
3. What have you done about those feelings? The problems initiating them?

Many ministers do more than think about quitting. Ten years ago the *Southern Baptist Convention Virginia Newspaper* reported, "Southern Baptist Convention clergy couples drop out of their churches on an average of 116 a month," due largely to the spouse's discontent.[3] Recent reports from the SBC show little improvement: nearly one hundred ministers are forced out of their churches each month.[4] Morale in the pastorate, it appears, is scraping bottom.

When low clergy morale results in pastoral turnover, the congregation suffers. Churches that frequently change pastors tend to be less open, less trusting and more inward looking, according to Barna Research.[5] Further, in times of turmoil and transition, attendance drops, giving declines, and lay leadership struggles may ensue.

Studies indicate that it takes years to truly see results in ministry with a new minister. Dr. Gary McIntosh cited research among several mainline denominations, which found that a pastor's most effective years in a pulpit don't even begin until the sixth or seventh year.[6] These are years that many ministers don't have. Dr. Thom Rainer, dean of the Billy Graham School of Missions, Evangelism and Church Growth of the Southern Baptist Theological Seminary in Louisville, states that the average tenure for all Protestant ministers is 2.3 years.[7]

With all the leaving, there's no time for cleaving, for forming mutually respectful relationships between the congregation and the ministry family. It can take at least five years in one pulpit for the pastor to gain the respect of constituents[8]—let alone see effective ministry happen.

Changing ministers takes its toll on both the clergy family and the local church. Unless a move is absolutely essential, clergy need to stay awhile longer for truly effective ministry to happen. Frequent moves disrupt the building process of ministry.

Real People, Real Pain, Real Problems

While we were in seminary, a professor warned us: "Congregations want to believe that their ministers and spouses are sinless and sexless." After years spent serving the local church, frustrated pastors and their mates echoed those feelings.

"I wonder if people in our congregation understand that we feel pain, anger and doubt just as they do," one pastor said. As for me, if asked how I felt that Sunday in church when I struggled in isolation with my grief, I would have answered, "Like

---

FACTS ON FILE

The pastor's "most pressing problems relate to time, money, and family."[9]

---

less than a human being, like my feelings and pain are insignif-
icant or nonexistent."

Laurie, in ministry in Oregon, said, "We who serve others
and serve them well may minister with broken hearts." Pastors
and families feel pain but are unsure what to do about it. Linda
and Mason worried what their congregation would think if
members knew their son was hospitalized for addiction treat-
ment for several weeks. When's Dan's father died, he couldn't
grieve as he needed because "I was concerned about keeping
my job."

Life in the pastorate is different from life in most homes.
Many professions are lonely, and ministry is no exception.
Hopefully, however, for most Christians church is where they
find support and sustenance. For the pastor the church is both
taskmaster and charge, and an awkward place to look for support and nourishment. The loneliness intensifies when parishioners hesitate to offer empathy. Perhaps they feel unqualified
or ineloquent. Perhaps, believing someone else is surely filling
that role in the cleric's life, they remain silent. Or perhaps they
are simply unaware that ministers need support.

Why the Clergy Family?
One report called pastors "the most occupationally frustrated
people in America."[10] That frustration has tremendous impact
on the family, because, as in few other careers, the spouse is
intimately tied to the minister's job. And with many leaving the
ministry because of the spouse's discontent, the ministry may
be only as strong as the marriage.

The same can be said about the pastor's family. Miserable
ministry children make the job doubly difficult for pastors.
Pastor, spouse, marriage and children: the suffering of one
skews the whole picture and hampers ministry. If all four are

cared for, the pastor will be energized and empowered for ministry.

Nurturing also enhances the minister's strength and resiliency. With lack of affirmation the most-cited reason for clergy burnout,[11] the congregation's thoughtful care of the pastor will lessen burnout's frequency. The length of time in each church will increase, and divorce, which is surprisingly high among pastors, will decrease when the pastor's marriage is honored. Fewer ministry children will feel alienated by the draining service of their parents in the local church. Nurturing the pastor's family may be the most amazing key to effectual churches and winning others to Christ.

Roy Oswald confirms this: "Our effectiveness as congregations in dealing with the pain and brokenness of our society is directly proportional to the congregation's health as a whole and the individual health of the clergy and its laity."[12]

Caring for the clergy is not a human-generated brainchild—some marketing whiz creating an event to sell more greeting cards. Nor is it another round of pop psychology or even church growth theory. It is plain common sense. It is also scriptural. God makes our responsibility toward those in ministry clear. In Deuteronomy the people are told, "Be careful not to neglect the Levites as long as you live in your land" (Deut 12:19). We are speaking, of course, of the New Testament corollary to the priests and Levites, the minister. The author of Hebrews commands the congregation: "Be responsive to your

---

FACTS ON FILE

Thirty-three percent of pastors leave churches due to conflicts with congregation, goals or expectations.[13]

---

pastoral leaders. . . . Contribute to the joy of their leadership not its drudgery. Why would you want to make things harder for them?" (Heb 13:17 The Message).

Stumbling Blocks to Caring

"Jane, could you call me back? I need to ask you a couple of questions." Grace's soft words on my recorder sounded tenuous. I always smiled at her messages. Most adept at caring for people, love for God radiates in her voice and her actions. When I called back, she explained her message.

"My uncle left me a small inheritance. Would you be offended if I bought some fun things for your family with part of my tithe? I've wanted to ask you for weeks but was afraid you'd be hurt."

I could hardly express my thanks. And Grace dropped off her purchases to ecstatic children. Boxes overflowed with lunchbox goodies and treats we couldn't afford. Truly she had followed the injunction in Hebrews, "Appreciate your pastoral leaders who gave you the Word of God" (Heb 13:7 The Message).

But even Grace, so gifted at caring for others, hesitated to ask if she could minister to us in this personal way. I have found others reluctant to offer help to their ministers and families too, largely because they fear offending. The only way past that fear is to do what Grace did: ask. Among the pastors I have spoken with, not one ever mentioned feeling put down by this kind of care.

Beyond fear of offending, a second stumbling block to caring for your minister and family is a lack of awareness of their needs. To learn how to support them, express a willingness to help. Ask how to best do that. As in any other relationship, a key to this is two-way communication.

FOR THE PASTOR
1. How do you communicate your needs to parishioners?
2. How do you best receive help?
3. How do you honestly feel about receiving help? For instance, "I have a hard time receiving help because . . ."

Getting Practical

Pulling our station wagon around to the front of a suburban church, I braked in surprise before the main entrance. An enormous banner, strung between two columns, flapped in the cutting November wind. In bold red letters, the message was clear: "We Love Our Pastors."

Inside, the women's coordinator who had invited me to speak welcomed me warmly. "I like your banner," I said casually.

The organizer smiled. "We're leaving it up for a bit longer. We want everyone to know what our pastors mean to us."

Later I asked one of their staff exactly how the congregation showed their love. A telling pause followed the question. Finally he answered, choosing words carefully:

"If someone sets an agenda to care for the minister, it happens. The banner, a result of Clergy Appreciation Month, is an example of that."

"But on a consistent basis?" I probed, a surgeon looking for signs of health—or illness. "How does the congregation care for you and your family?"

Again, words trailed a long silence. "If you want to be nice to someone, be nice to the people they love. When someone cares for my family, I feel loved. But out of two hundred families, only one or two people give my wife special attention on her birthday."

When Moses' arms grew too tired to raise over Israel, others came alongside and held up their leader's arms so that Israel might continue to win the battle before them. When judicial leadership overwhelmed Moses, God provided seventy people to assist him. Whether physically, emotionally or spiritually, when we honor and support the person God has called into ministry, we honor God.

In the following pages, pastors and their families graciously share their joy, their pain and their hope. Helpful ideas, studies for small groups or Sunday school classes and other hints will prepare us to honor and care for the clergy family.

And that care can begin as soon as the moving van pulls away and the new occupants throw the welcome mat on the stoop.

Keeping the Pastor We Love

Where do I sense my minister is overwhelmed? What would it be like to reverse pastoral care and care for the pastor?

How can I offer compassion and comfort when clergy face difficulties and heartaches? How will I know what they are facing?

In what ways can I express appreciation and gratitude for the pastor's work?

Here is how I will begin to pray for my minister (see appendix A for ideas):

2

The Welcome Mat

Open wide your hearts.

2 CORINTHIANS 6:13

Within days of burying his parents, Rev. Seymour accepted a call to a new church in a new community. In six weeks, this pastor from Boston would leave behind thirteen years of relationships and associations. "It's almost as hard to leave as it is to bear the unexpected deaths of my parents." This ministry family was torn from the only place they'd known as home; here they had ushered their son from kindergarten through high school graduation. The roots were deep—as was the pain of leaving.

Research on moving indicates that men are better able to plunge into work and less likely to feel the pain of moving. However, conversations with pastors did not bear out the research. I found both men and women clergy grieving the loss of relationships. When Jamie served Communion to church members the final time, tears streamed down her cheeks. With Randall's move imminent, he ached over the people he would leave—relationships severed—even as he anticipated the new life emerging—relationships to be formed.

Regardless of profession, moving is painful for people. The pastoral family is no exception.

Ministers Talk About Moving

"What makes you groan at the thought of moving to a new church?" I asked pastors in phone interviews.

"The price I pay in being highly visible in many places so the congregation will begin to trust me, then free me for my area of specialty," said one minister. "It's hard on me and hard on my family."

"What makes me groan? Learning everyone's names and going through the 'honeymoon period' of being all things to all people," said another pastor.

"Unpacking," stated a clergy member from Tennessee. "Unpacking and knowing that the second I arrive the congregation will pile expectations upon me."

One minister acknowledged, "Not being able to take time to settle in. In one church, two years passed before I unpacked my books and arranged my office functionally. I had to plunge in immediately."

Allen, a minister from El Paso, said, "All the change is stressful. Inadequate housing, having my wife quit her job, the accompanying loss of income and mediating in a difficult situation. . . . It's almost too much."

On top of these, pastors worried about spouses and children adapting to all the newness: home, church, expectations, schools, friends, clubs, sports. They also felt anxiety about helping their families through the stress and grief of major up-

heaval. It may take as long as two years to work through relocation struggles. Further, pastors who move frequently do not
grow past the startup stages of ministry. This, plus the cost of
broken relationships, plus the toll on a church in transition,
and the final bill skyrockets.

Grief Observed

When the empty moving van roars away from the new parsonage or home, far more is left in the cloud of exhaust than heavy
boxes and furniture. Those in ministry heft more extensive bag-
gage than labeled brown cartons. In the weeks of packing and
moving, they have also packed away grief, loss and loneliness.
While excessive busyness may camouflage these feelings during
the first weeks at a new church, before long the trio will raise
their collective heads and begin an uneasy, mournful howl.

Few pastors come through a move without grief. Freedom to
grieve is vital to recovery and will aid future ministry in the
new church. Failure to grieve compromises that very ministry.

After one move, Rev. Leithner of Oklahoma journaled the
poem "Moving Day."

Moving Day

Rooted up, tearing my hand from the door,
my eyes from familiar faces,
my heart from its home,
there is no time for tears.
The Trail rolls gently north
but it has not been a gentle day,
No.

The sun beat the coolness away early
before dreams and dew.
We trucked our worldly goods with weary arms.

I cannot weep and drive at once
so I drive.

It is 104° while we unload,
new people to meet
offering arms to share the sweat.
I cannot weep and meet new friends at once
so I meet new friends.

Mammoth stacks of unpacked boxes
cleaning, painting, fixing
I cannot weep and unpack at once
so I unpack.

A sermon to prepare,
hands to shake, introductions to make
in the same days as unpacking.
I cannot weep and type and preach at once
so I type and preach.

Empty boxes to fold and store,
full ones yet to open,
pictures unhung, files unfiled, notes unwritten.
And I cannot weep and store and hang at once
so I store and hang.

When, oh Lord, when
when will there be a time
for this grief ignored,
this sorrow delayed
these tears unwept
to be released . . .

when will there be time for tears?[1]

Heavy Losses

Grief is just one of the many facets of moving that families face.
Our culture narrows grief to a cursory definition: mourning over

someone's death. However, grief in a broader sense is about loss: loss of friends, community, identity, and the loss of dreams and expectations. This totals an enormous emotional energy loss.[2]

"I left part of myself behind when I moved," Gill, a pastor in an urban church, sighed. "I invested heavily in church relationships. Now I have to begin again."

"Losses?" said Steve. "I've lost a decade of my history with a community. My past is a closed book that few here will ever open or read."

"Seeing people come to Christ and then develop from 'babies' to mature Christians is the greatest part of ministry," said Debbie. "A move deflates that entire sense of being in a family from the beginning."

Carol, a clergy spouse, experienced complete identity loss in her new church. "I couldn't take my résumé with me when we moved. The volunteer work, the hours invested in the community, the time spent creating a job for myself—gone. I started again from scratch. It's like annihilation."

Moving depletes creative energy, a huge deficit for both pastor and family. Tearing apart a home saps a family's strength. Lynn, a minister's wife and author, says that "every time I move I lose a year of my life and barely write a word." It's as powerful a loss as cutting off Samson's hair.

No Roots

One major impact of moving is rootlessness. Research shows that families move an average of every 6 years. As we have seen, clergy statistics are more sobering, averaging from 2.3 to 4 years in one spot. One pastor, forty-six, also a pastor's child and now in his current church seven years, shakes his head. "It's the longest I've ever lived in one house in my whole life."

Moving is a fact of life. But not only do pastors move more

frequently, with the turn of a key they close the door on job, community, friends. They have packed their memories into boxes that few will open. And they are moving into a home, a church and a social circle already chosen for them, in which they will find few true friends.

No church shopping, no weekend sleep-ins to recuperate from the stress of change. In the new situation they are always on call, always a role model, always expected. Other professionals' spouses may be freed of any expectations except acclimating the family and household to a new location and routine. But in a new church, clergy spouses may instantly be handed a mantle of expectations that they are not ready to wear.

"We leave one place and arrive at another the same day. One Sunday we say good-bye, the next hello, and in between we undergo radical transplant surgery without recovery time," writes Rev. Leithner.[3]

Ministry is a building process. Exiting one church and entering another creates a complete loss of momentum for the pastor, leaving a void easily filled by discouragement and sometimes despair. Roy Oswald, in *Clergy Self-Care,* warns that anyone under excessive strain needs more rest and sleep. This is especially true during transitions into a new job or role.[4]

With a little effort, churches can give pastoral families the recovery time they need to thrive. Pastors tend to jump into new positions up to their necks during that "honeymoon period" of first six to twelve months. Slowing them down and helping

---

FACTS ON FILE

The average tenure of associate ministers and staff is less than two years.[5]

---

them take care of home life and personal grieving make the transition easier.

Processing the losses of a move is personal business. Perhaps the best way the congregation can assist is to provide necessary time for the minister to acclimate to the new church, suspending expectations and reaching out as friends.

FOR THE PASTOR

1. Meditate on Deuteronomy 31:8: "The LORD himself goes before you and will be with you; he will never leave you nor forsake you. Do not be afraid; do not be discouraged." When do you most experience the presence of God going before you?
2. In what ways can you invite the Lord's presence?
3. When you feel afraid or discouraged, what factors contribute to those feelings? What do you do with them?

Loneliness

Loneliness sweeps in on the heels of grief and loss. The loss of friends is one of the heaviest sustained in the front lines of a move. Louis McBurney, in *Clergy Couples in Crisis,* says ministers feel "dislodged and not belonging" after a move; loneliness and pressure are common.[6] Close relationships take three years or more to establish.

Pastors and families are typically expected to sever ties with the former congregation. For the sake of the incoming clergy, there should be a clean break in authority so loyalty is not divided and growth compromised. The new minister deserves that respect. No running back and forth, attending worship services, comparing notes, splitting the camp.

Still, the former church represented worship, work, validation, self-esteem and community to the departing pastor and family. Severing all ties is like hacking a bush off at ground level and poking it into a new hole someplace else. If roots are to grow from that cutting, they come only as a result of water, nourishment and warm soil pressed firmly around the trunk. The congregation is well equipped and divinely appointed to handle the time-consuming process.

What Can We Do?

Think about practical gestures to offer during those first few weeks. The biggest hurdle on arrival at the parsonage or new house, according to many clergy, was finding it uninhabitable: needing repairs and deep cleaning before they could unload or unpack. One pastor moving in discovered the house had no attic and had standing water in the basement. Most of us clean our homes for company; having the house or manse ready for the pastor is an enormous gesture of hospitality.

I met Kathy when my husband interviewed for the pastoral position at her church. Two days after our move she appeared to help unpack. Having someone tear off newspaper and collapse boxes was a tremendous relief. Kathy became a prayer partner and dear friend—all because of that initial opening of her heart. Helping hands tangibly symbolize warm, open spirits.

One pastor's wife wept remembering the crew of women who called and said, "We'd like to come over and help you get settled. Would that be okay? When is a good time?"

A minister talked softly as if holding back emotion. "The church people cared about me. They wanted to know how to help, what things I'd miss the most about our last church. I felt like a real person. They gave me permission to be vulnerable."

For more ideas on helping when your pastor moves in, see "Move-In Checklist" in appendix F.

HONORING THE PASTOR'S MOVE

■ Create a welcome packet, listing parks, cinemas, bargain shops, doctors, major grocery stores, free activities, fun (affordable) restaurants. Janet made such a list for me, and at the bottom included her own phone number, adding, "Please use it often."

■ Treat the new family to one of those great eateries. How nice for them to not have to cook and eat a meal on top of unpacked boxes.

■ The first few weeks are not easy for socials, but organizing a cookout after that time at your home would nourish newcomers.

■ Help the minister understand unwritten rules. Expectations for pastors in rural communities will differ from those in an urban or suburban area. (One clergyman rode the tractor with his parishioners! Imagine the urban transplant faced with that expectation.)

■ Learn the names of the family, and find out their likes and dislikes. Surprise them with their favorite takeout meal, or deliver a pizza to their door.

■ Fresh flowers make a lovely welcome splurge.

■ Consider a gift certificate to the hardware or wallpaper store. Resettling eats up huge chunks of a pastor's first paychecks. "We spend about $1000 after every move making the new house work," wrote Melissa.

■ Theater passes or a restaurant menu with a gift certificate send the message, "We respect your privacy as well as your need for a break, and we love you."

■ A get-started kitchen box—towels, potholders and a first meal's fixins would be a pack anyone would welcome.

■ How about a phone card and a note mentioning the need to connect with loved ones left behind?

Each pastoral family is different. Asking, "How can I help during this time?" and "Where are you overwhelmed?" will warm numbed souls. Acknowledging the difficulties of a clergy move and being available in the aftershock of uprooting will strengthen the budding relationship. Time to settle, feel and heal is a wonderful welcome-home gift.

Psalm 23 speaks of preparing a banquet "in the presence of my enemies." If the enemies of relocation are grief, loss and loneliness, the church can be in the foxhole with the pastoral family. Sometimes we can prepare a literal banquet: food, meals, staples for the pantry. The church can be God's instruments to get clergy families through the frontline bullets that always attack in transition's dark valley.

Learning to be present without answers in the midst of the

pain is one of the great gifts the body of Christ can offer. Writes Karen Mains in her book *Friends and Strangers,* "Rarely are any of us given the gift of sincere interest. Something tender, something gentle happens when this gift is given. Christ comes near."[7]

A month after we moved in, Sandy pulled up to our curb. Rich and I were sorting through hastily packed boxes, hoping to squeeze a car into the garage. Ruthie and Zak flitted around our kneecaps and the open door of the house, as did the flies.

"Hello, folks!" Sandy's now-familiar voice boomed. The children stopped flitting and looked interested. "How about if I take your young'uns out for a kiddie meal while you two concentrate here?" We were relieved, the kids were thrilled, and our hearts grew wider because of her care.

Welcome to (Y)Our Church

Feeling welcomed in a new home and new neighborhood is one thing, but for many children (and some clergy spouses), the prospect of hundreds of blank, unfamiliar faces staring at them in the church halls and sanctuary is terrifying. To ease the terror, one church had a welcome reception between services, and the children's choir presented music they'd practiced for weeks. Our preschoolers felt instant rapport with the children's singing and relaxed visibly.

On the surface the minister's kids are no different from other children in the congregation. There are, however, differing underlying dynamics, which will be discussed more deeply in a future chapter. For starters, the church is picked for them. So welcoming the children is like water and fertilizer around the roots in easing transplant difficulties for the entire family. It's important to note, however, that some pastors' children would prefer to slip in unnoticed; maybe they want to be known simply as "Bill and Susie" rather than as "the new pastor's children." Checking with the parents first will help a church or group decide exactly how to proceed.

Kids, including ministry children, need structure. Change, especially the wholesale change of a move, is difficult on everyone. Please be tolerant of an irritable, shy or clingy child. And don't feel bad if the kids won't stay in the nursery, don't like Sunday school right away or skip youth group; it takes time and patience to adjust and find the right niche for each person.

Ministers appreciate it during those first stranger-weeks when someone approaches, offers a handshake and reminds them of his or her name. Who wins the "I'll bet you can't remember my name" game, anyway? Nametags are another possibility at the beginning of a pastor's ministry. Though they may seem impersonal, for the early weeks after a move nametags are very helpful. Getting a picture directory to new pastors immediately aids them in pairing faces and names.

Many Options, One Goal
Whether it's a hot meal or a warm hug, a helping hand or a ready ear, making the transition as gracious and painless as possible for new clergy infinitely speeds recovery. When it's time to shake out the welcome mat, wide hearts, space and practical help are powerful frontline defenses against loneliness, grief and loss. And as in every relationship, communication will prove vital in caring for the minister and family.

Keeping the Pastor We Love
What stories have I heard about the new ministry family's moving experience? (Have I asked?)

How can I help allow time so the pastor can unpack and settle in before assuming responsibilities?

Have I done my grief work well surrounding the departing minister so I can more easily reach out to the new one?

What do I know about the minister's previous years in ministry? Can I open the history books and get to know them better?

How can I open my heart and life to the pastor and family?

What can I do to help the pastor's children feel welcome and accepted in their new church?

Here is how I will pray for my minister:

3

Communication
in the Church

*If it is possible, as far as it depends on you,
live at peace with everyone.*

ROMANS 12:18

For nearly three years, Neil served First Church as head pastor. This southern California church initially hired him as the associate, a position he filled for five years. The search committee, after lengthy interviewing and a vote, brought on a second minister, Terry.

Neil introduced Terry to First Church with grace and friendliness, investing much time in establishing a good working relationship. When the board deemed the training complete, they said, "Thanks, Neil. Now you'll be the associate pastor again, and Terry will be the senior pastor."

Neil was floored and deeply wounded. No one had told him that Terry would be the senior pastor, that he was training his own replacement. After years of faithful work, trust was broken. It took much time and prayer to find healing for Neil and his family and to enable them to continue at First Church. He chose to stay rather than tear away at the fabric of God's work over the past years by leaving, but not all clergy make that choice.

By one estimate, most forced terminations result from about seven people with their own agendas for the church, which do not line up with the pastor's view or method.[1] Some call this "ecclesiastical violence." If 40 percent of pastors resign due to church conflict; if 47 percent leave ministry entirely because of superhuman but unwritten expectations and overwhelming job descriptions;[2] if one-third of clergy will be forced from their church during their careers[3]—then we must ask whether God-honoring communication is happening in the church.

Assumptions

Assumptions may have been one problem with Neil's situation. An assumption is not communication. By definition, *communication* refers to transferring information, thought or feeling so that it is satisfactorily received or understood. An assumption doesn't even fulfill the transferring requirement.

At First Church, perhaps the elders and search committee assumed that Neil knew Terry was replacing the previous pastor. Perhaps Neil assumed, having functioned well as head pastor for those years, that logically he would continue in the position and the incoming pastor would be the associate.

Most likely, the elders didn't consciously deceive Neil while laboriously seeking another pastor. Most likely, there was no deliberate underhandedness. But it would have been so much better to eliminate assumptions by talking things through up front so no one was deceived or wounded!

If we do get beyond assumptions to uttering words, many of us stop there. We said it, that should settle it. We don't check out whether the other person heard what we said or meant, or how they felt about what we said. We hit "send" but never know if "receive" happens.

Another problem with so-called communication is that, often, we don't want to hear from the other party. We just want our piece said, our agenda completed, our feelings ejected. It isn't communication; it's hit and run. Sadly, this happens in our churches as well as our homes and communities.

A parishioner approached the pastor just before a warm time of worship began. For weeks, she'd lugged around anger toward him, and in front of the congregation she released a round of fiery verbiage. The pastor apologized for the misunderstanding, then said, "This is not the best time, perhaps, to discuss this. Could we finish clearing it up later?" The layperson smiled thinly, launched in again with venom and left.

A rock can derail a train. A pig (or deer) can total a car. And poor communication can destroy the church. When we are open to dialogue rather than a bomb drop and our hearts are in the right place, we are ready to communicate. How we communicate is as important as what we communicate.

FOR THE PASTOR
1. How do you feel about the level of conflict and communication in the church?
2. How do you handle conflict? What does it do to your blood pressure?
3. How do you pray for the conflicted?

How Do We Want to Communicate?

With compassion. Compassion is sympathetic awareness of another's distress, with a desire to alleviate that distress. This is a missing piece in much of our communication, living and ministry together. We may feel bad about something in another's life but not have the slightest interest in easing or removing the pain or problem from them. How does this fit in with the life rule "Love your neighbor as yourself"?

Understanding we are complementary. We all fit together to make one whole; none of us is dispensable or disposable. Not me, not you, not the pastor, not the youth minister, the neighbor, the Christian education director, the nursery helper, the person folding bulletins. We must learn to work together, to compensate for another's weakness, to alleviate suffering and pain where possible, to make allowances for one another.

In community. Community literally means with unity. As a unified body of individuals—community defined—we are to live together. Too often the church is like mega tug of war, each person or committee or group pulling for personal agendas. (One pastor said, "I feel like the rope.") In these adult-sized games, we forget the point of the church: to grow up into maturity like Christ, sharing Christ with an unbelieving, hurting, lost world.

Unity is key. A group of people working for the same end equals power, as we saw at Babel. The entire gathering of individuals, all speaking the same language, decided to work together. Great! The problem? Their goal was to build a tower to heaven, to be God. And so God took them apart, scattered them, scrambled their languages, knowing that power used toward the wrong ends destroys. We cannot afford to function without unity in our community.

As a compassionate, complementary community, we are ready to communicate.

Good Communication

Romans 12 gives excellent how-tos for living—communicating—in community. One pastor's spouse from Utah wrote, "I live in a world of 'backdoor' conversations, backhanded comments, innuendoes and manipulations. I just want people to say what they mean and mean what they say. When I am talking with someone, I say what I mean, and it makes me insane when people try to 'read' into what I am trying to say."

This is not honest love; this does not follow with Paul's admonition that "love must be sincere" (Rom 12:9). Another translation renders it "without hypocrisy." Hypocrisy is rooted in a theater term meaning "speaking or acting under a false part; pretending or feigning."[4] We are to drop all pretense and love honestly.

Back to Mercy

These characteristics are impossible without God's mercies as our backdrop (see Romans 11). Knowing we are incapable of loving sincerely, we throw ourselves on God's mercy and empowerment. In this position of humility, we are prepared to speak the truth in love. Because we know how imperfect we are, we can say to another, "I need to talk with you." This leaves no room for anger, blame or shame. Out of humility and hospitality, understanding the vital importance of each member in our community, we can lovingly speak the truth to another.

To speak the truth in love, we first communicate that

LOVE MUST BE SINCERE
Read through Romans 12 and meditate on some of the internal and external characteristics of sincere love . . .

GODWARD
■ Live holy and pleasing lives inwardly
■ Be transformed
■ Renew our minds
■ Don't have inflated views of ourselves

OUTWARD
■ Remember that we each have our own function and gifts
■ Be devoted to one another
■ Honor one another above ourselves
■ Never be lacking in zeal
■ Joyful in hope
■ Be patient in affliction
■ Be faithful in prayer
■ Share with God's people
■ Practice hospitality
■ Bless those who persecute us
■ Live in harmony with one another
■ Do not be proud
■ Live at peace with everyone

love. Jesus came full of grace and truth. Truth alone can destroy. But grace and truth together bring others closer to God and the church closer together. We communicate our love for another by faithfulness in prayer, hospitality, helping the other in need, blessing instead of cursing, serving instead of hurting.

When people want to communicate they usually mean "I have a bone to pick with you." Or a to-do list for you. Or a major problem you need to take care of. Or a favor to ask. What about first communicating some of these:

☐ praise
☐ appreciation
☐ prayer
☐ support
☐ understanding
☐ love
☐ acceptance
☐ friendship
☐ forgiveness
☐ commitment

Going in Circles

Communication is circular. It starts with asking God to renew our minds about the state of our own souls and about God's mercy and love; reaching out to others with that same mercy and love and acceptance; making certain our talking equals our listening and our listeners receive the correct message; listening to the other person; and beginning again in humility and self-examination and repentance.

Doesn't leave much room for conflict, does it? Because we always check out the reception, always listen with our whole hearts, always believe the best, always work through misunderstandings—why, there's no room for argument! No room for ugliness. No room for dishonesty and blame and self-centered agendas.

Because communication is about peace.

Committees and the Church Hotline

These are nice principles about good communication. However, they don't exactly gel with many committee and church experiences. Some would say that committees are notorious for their unbusinesslike, unspiritual approach to the doings of the church. Assumptions and hidden expectations pollute the air. Backdoor deals. Salem witch trials. One committee, thirteen members, thirteen agendas. Often it's "Get the meeting over with," not necessarily "Get God's work done."

SHORTCUTS TO
COMMUNICATION
- Love first.
- Believe the best.
- Go in humility.
- Be willing to be wrong.
- Speak the truth.
- Invite response.
- Listen carefully.
- Love some more.
- Live at peace with one another

At one church a layperson wanted a key leadership position but did not tell the committee her desires. She had held various roles for a decade but was gone five months a year. The committee did not inform her that they were looking for new leadership who could give more consistent nurture to groups. The committee and the layperson were angry, and no resolution occurred.

At another church the board of elders was fragmented and furious. Linda, their pastor, asked for silence and prayer around the table to listen to God. Finally, one elder prayed aloud, repenting of the destructive anger. The tender confession opened the others' hearts, and unity began to take root. "Let every one be quick to hear, slow to speak and slow to anger; for . . . anger . . . does not achieve the righteousness of God" (Jas 1:19-20 NASB).

The flash-fire effect of the church hotline is dramatic as well. One pastor stepped away from the pulpit at the end of the worship service. Her voice held a warning tone. "For your information: I am still happily married; I am not buying a house with the realtor; I am not leaving the ministry. For those of you who started the rumors and spread the rumors, I forgive you. Next time there's a question, ask me. Though no one asked, I will tell you: the realtor and I were looking at the house near the church hoping we could expand the church property." Faces reddened and heads tipped down. After the service, a woman approached the minister at the door, nearly overcome with contrition. "I was one of the people who believed the rumors. Please forgive me."

Collin and Heidi experienced the same gossip mill, though with tragic results. Returning from a renewal event for ministry couples, they caught wind of a rumor that they were leaving the church. Some parishioners had met secretly to figure out how to get rid of them. It took only five months for the group of seven to oust their head pastor.

Knowing the church's needs is vital when hiring; faithfully keeping that covenant is crucial to carrying out God's will in that church and community. Being honest—loving without hypocrisy—in the process is key.

Twenty-five percent of churches have more than one pastor on staff[5]; inter-staff conflict is familiar to many of those churches. Having staff open to God's transformation must be characteristic of each member.

Fred was the wrong guy in the top spot. An introvert, his idea of community was reading alone. His staff begged him for staff retreats, for relationship, for spiritual accountability between ministers. His inability to be in relationship destroyed the staff. They resigned, demoralized and rejected.

A clergy spouse from Kansas said, "We walk on egg shells around the senior pastor and spouse. They feel very threatened by us for some reason. We never know if we're going to be snubbed, punished or watched for something."

This conflicts with God's call on each of us to "grow in love," to be transformed, to be open to God shaping us through interaction with one another. Church staffs and boards can facilitate these qualities by continuing to call one another back to God's mission for the church and heart for the world. When we're all working for the same right goal (remember Babel!) there is no room for competition between Christ's people. James asks, "What is the source of quarrels and conflicts among you?" and points out, "Where jealousy and selfish ambition exist, there is disorder and every evil thing" (Jas 4:1; 3:16 NASB).[6]

Keeping dialogue moving on committees will also avoid the festering and fracturing so prevalent in churches today. One conflict-avoidant pastor shushed any trouble. When he left, the people learned that he had kept hidden a parishioner's history of child molestation and the abuse of a child from the church. The abuser still attended the church.

Honesty is always better. "I'd rather be socked in the nose than stabbed in the back," said one pastor. "We've had some rocky and uncomfortable times, sorting through issues, but we work it out."

What About Confrontation?
What about Scriptures like Leviticus 19:17: "Rebuke your neighbor frankly so you will not share in his guilt"? That passage begins, "Do not hate your brother in your heart." That's a

good start. Of course there are times when we must communicate difficult truth with another. Peacemaking requires addressing problems before they become conflicts. So many problems are built on misunderstandings. Mike Miller says, "Most churches have more policies for weddings, flowers and custodial needs than they do for dealing with conflict between the minister and the church. Failure to talk about this issue has made it worse."[7]

Establishing a chain of contact helps. This does not mean gripe to the pastor's spouse about the pastor or grouse to a neighbor. Nor does it mean write a poisonous letter to the chair of the staff relations committee or the elders. Nor do we go first to the denominational head or the district superintendent. Confrontation is not filling someone with verbal buckshot or destroying another's reputation by spouting to the wrong person. Where is the peace in this? This is irresponsible behavior. Scripture calls it sin.

Jesus commands that if we have an issue with another, we first talk alone with that person. If the other doesn't listen, we bring a friend (who displays all the characteristics we've discussed) with us. If that does not help, we take the matter to a board, then to the church (Mt 18:15-17). Taking these steps makes a community-wide blow-up and confrontation much less likely.

FOR THE PASTOR
1. What most angers you right now in your church?
2. Write down your own failures and shortcomings in the situation.
3. Find mercy.
4. When have you broken the chain of contact or forgotten the peace way?
5. What happened?
6. How do you challenge your congregation, or a grouser, to move toward high-end, Christlike communication?

Robert's church set up a chain of contact by appointing an elder to function as a liaison between church, board and Robert himself. This gentleman defuses inflammatory situations and handles communication problems and questions, interpreting situations for both parties. Functioning much as an armor bearer in the Old Testament, he has become not only an advocate for the pastor but also a tried and true friend, standing in the gap and facilitating godly relationships between minister, staff and church.

Healing the Wounded

Perhaps you or your church has wounded someone in ministry. If so, please do not carry guilt any longer. Confess this to one another and to the persons you have harmed. Ask for forgiveness. If the wounded cannot forgive, invite them to talk about their pain with you, to detail how you hurt them. Knowing what has been received is part of the communication circle as well. Pray for the persons harmed. God does not take it lightly when the body of Christ hurts the people who have been appointed and anointed for ministry in the church.

Make My Joy Complete

Good communication begins with our relationship with Christ. Our unity with him and the comfort received from being loved sets us free to love one another faithfully, so that life may be found in our words.

> If you have any encouragement from being united with Christ, if any comfort from his love, if any fellowship with the Spirit, if any tenderness and compassion, then make my joy complete by being like-minded, having the same love, being one in spirit and

purpose. Do nothing out of selfish ambition or vain conceit, but in humility consider others better than yourselves. Each of you should look not only to your own interests, but also to the interests of others. (Phil 2:1-4)

The church that loves like this need never worry about attrition and problems of pastoral turnover. And they'll be able to keep the pastor they love. And the world, longing for that love, will say, "See how they love one another!"

Keeping the Pastor We Love

What assumptions have I made about our local church and about my pastor? How—and whom—have those assumptions harmed? Benefited?

When have I seen compassion, complementarity and community lived out? How can I portray these qualities toward my minister?

How have I failed others? Make a list.

Devotion, honor, patience, zeal, hope . . . how am I living out these qualities?

What could I say to communicate praise, appreciation and understanding to my pastor?

How has my pastor failed me? How should I address this so it doesn't take root as bitterness?

Here's how I will pray for my minister:

GUIDELINES FOR BETTER CHURCH-TO-PASTOR COMMUNICATION
- Be honest about expectations.
- Communicate unwritten rules about the church and parsonage. (If the coffee pot is an idol, tell the ministerial family so they don't unwittingly use it for a social or for the staff barbecue at the manse.)
- Write down the unwritten rules.
- Be willing to negotiate on those rules!
- Get the job description and benefits/compensation package in print.
- Ask questions to clarify.
- Assume nothing.

4

Beyond the Sunday Sermon

Dear friends, let us love one another, for love comes from God. . . .
Since God so loved us, we also ought to love one another.
No one has ever seen God; but if we love one another,
God lives in us and his love is made complete in us.

1 JOHN 4:7, 11-12

Smiling at the secretary and greeting a parishioner, the minister walked slowly into his office and shut the door. He braced his back against the cool wood and turned the key. With slumped shoulders, this Georgia pastor settled into his chair; his heaviness belied his thin frame. Like every other day that week, he dropped his head on his forearms and wept.

The pastorate has fallen into disfavor. From Hollywood to Capitol Hill, ministry is no longer a highly esteemed position. And it shows in the faces, postures and spirits of many clergy.

Assimilating the results of a comprehensive survey of Protestant ministers, George Barna of Barna Research Group refused to accept the harsh reality. Instead he retraced his methodology twice more, collecting insights from a total of 1,033 senior ministers. The results did not vary. Pastors in America are troubled.

At the Brownsville Assembly of God in Pensacola, Florida, ministers from all over America assembled for a pastors' conference in the 1990s. A steady stream of America's finest spoke of trials experienced in ministry. For many, this conference was life or death. They had crawled through a desert hoping for a drink.

What contributes to the arid condition of ministers' souls? And how can the average layperson in the average church help?

Spiritual Drought
In talking with clergy from across North America, a similar theme appeared.

"I love reading Scripture, praying, teaching others about Jesus," said Joe, a pastor in Cincinnati. "When God called me to the ministry, I thought I could do what I love full time and support myself."

Joe's voice dropped to a sad, haunting note. "I don't know when I last read the Bible for my own spiritual life."

Many pastors are overwhelmed not by people's love and appreciation (1 Thess 5:12-13) but by the demands of the job—

FACTS ON FILE

Forty percent of pastors doubt their present church experience significantly deepens their own relationship with Christ.

Sixty percent say that their experience at their present church has not greatly increased their passion for ministry.[1]

---

many of which could be shared by laypeople. Pastors often lack opportunities for personal development when they carry the laity's share of ministry.[2]

Massachusetts' clergy ranked spiritual dryness as the most common ministry problem.[3] Barbara Gilbert in *Who Ministers to Ministers?* states, "Spiritual dryness . . . tops the list of personal issues for male clergy."[4]

The problem, while easy to rank, is not as easy to solve. Never-ending demands and crises in ministers' days edge out necessary time for spiritual disciplines, for the first love that wooed them into the pastorate. How then can the pastors provide stable, sound spiritual modeling and leadership for the church?

"I need some off-duty time. I need an emotional sabbath."[5] This pastor's cry echoes those of ministers the world over.

Notice a page from history: "Very early in the morning, while it was still dark, Jesus got up, left the house and went off to a solitary place, where he prayed" (Mk 1:35). This is doubly strategic considering what Jesus' "sabbath" looked like the day before: he taught, exorcised demons, healed Simon's mother-in-law, and when the sun went down "the whole town gathered at the door" (1:33). If the Author of our faith—the Lord of the sabbath—needed a spiritual sabbath for replenishment, how much more do our pastors?

According to the Alban Institute, most clergy average over sixty hours of work per week. By then, the law of diminishing returns kicks in, because work quality declines after fifty hours. None of the ministers I've spoken with, read about or know personally consistently take their allocated one day off per week. Some pastors couldn't remember the last day entirely free of church business. For most, there is no day of sabbath rest, and certainly not the five-day workweek common to many North Americans.

Ironically, it was the director of a funeral home who asked my husband, "Why don't pastors take two days off? They don't get a weekend, but what about a two-day block during the week?"

One day a week scarcely suffices for clergy or anyone to recharge emotionally, physically and spiritually; keep one's home in order and in repair; and have quality and quantity family time. Ministers do not move from glory to glory but from crisis to crisis. Even if they took their one allotted day off, it is not enough to keep them from becoming one of those untimely funerals.

William, a Canadian pastor, worked out with his supervising elder a life-giving and revolutionary system. William tracks workdays, the days off he uses and those he can't take off because of church demands. Each month, he and the elder log the compensation days accrued—the days William couldn't take off. Comp days are his to take at another time, either in lump sum or one by one.

In a board meeting William outlined his vacation days for the upcoming quarter. "Wait," one elder protested. "This seems like far more than allowed for vacation time."

The supervising elder explained William's accountability for those comp days. A triple benefit occurred: William did not have to leap to his own defense but, supported by his elder, felt built up; the church gained greater understanding of the minister's needs and schedule; and William could take the time not only due him but so necessary to soul and body and family life.

Part of the Solution

Rather than add to the problem, the church can be part of the solution to the drought in a minister's experience. Writes George Barna:

The time has come for the laity to be more sensitive to the spiritual needs and development of their leaders. . . . It is foolish to expect an individual who is not growing spiritually to competently and passionately lead others to grow spiritually. . . . This is an area that most congregations need to address immediately; to delay . . . can only bring further harm to the body itself.[6]

But ministers must also choose growth for themselves. Note the correlation between the state of a pastor's soul and the life of the congregation in Jeremiah 31:14 (NASB): "'I will fill the soul of the priests with abundance, and My people shall be satisfied with My goodness,' declares the LORD."

"The way to keep a congregation vital is to be a vital, growing person in their midst," says church consultant Roy Oswald. "Clergy don't need more knowledge or skills as much as they need a deeper spiritual life."[7]

Pastors are, in the final analysis, responsible for their own growth. Still, when congregations understand the state of ministers' souls, they can practice encouraging them spiritually.

FOR THE PASTOR
E. M. Bounds states, "The character of our praying will determine the character of our preaching. Light praying will make light preaching. Prayer makes preaching strong, gives it unction, and makes it stick."[8]
1. How well do you practice the process of prayer and then preaching? Think of the times when you felt "unction," that old-fashioned word underscoring the divine anointing as you deliver God's word to the people. Do you long for them again? What will you allow to hinder the necessary soul care to be able to preach "with unction"?
2. Who keeps you on track spiritually so that you take care of your soul? What accountability do you have?

The Omniscience Quotient: Expectations and the Pastorate
"You didn't come to see my mother while she was so ill." The woman's eyes burned holes into Rev. Stewart. "Where were

you when we needed you?"

The pastor's voice was low, gentle. "Alice, when did you tell me she was in the hospital?"

Alice dropped her gaze, mumbling, "You should know. I—I thought you knew."

WATER ON A THIRSTY LAND:
How the Church Can Revitalize
the Soul

■ Offer to stop in and pray with and for the pastor weekly.

■ Create a framework for clergy and staff, making a five-day workweek possible.

■ Encourage your ministers to track comp days; help keep them accountable for their use of "weekends."

■ Find out what settings most nourish your pastors, and arrange to get them there regularly. One resort owner lets his pastor spend a day there each week.

■ Book and pay for a room for the pastor in a retreat center one overnight a month, or three or four times a year.

■ Arrange for a six-week sabbatical with pay every four years for the minister; make all pulpit-supply arrangements; don't expect your clergy to pay for pulpit-supply or the on-call pastors (see appendix C, "Sabbaticals and Renewal Leaves").

■ Ensure that the pastor takes every week of vacation time (experts suggest a minimum of three weeks for people in caregiving fields).

■ Just plain fun is life-giving. Consider ways to inject fun into the seriousness of ministry.

The minister, who often acts as a lightning rod, was a likely target for Alice's pain over her mother's death. Her anger, which steamrolled to the point of threatening Rev. Stewart's pastorate, began to dissipate through conversations with the pastor and the pastor-relations board.

Somewhere, a universal, unwritten expectation exists: that pastors have a direct, intuitive crisis line revealing the problems and needs of parishioners. These hidden assumptions have led to pastoral depression and guilt, and result in conflict in many churches.

"One of the most frustrating and enraging bits of church life for me was that people expected me to read their minds," said Mark who, after thirteen years in ministry, left to pursue his doctorate in teaching. "If my Omniscience Quotient was down for that day, I was in trouble."

When my husband was considering a call to another church, we reviewed the job description. I actually laughed. My response: "Cut the job description in half, invite them to hire two people, pick the part that best suits your gifts and calling, and see what happens." Matching the pastor's primary gifts and the congregation's primary needs, then divvying up the remaining responsibilities between laypeople assures that the jobs will be fulfilled fairly.

Two people working sixty hours a week could not have fulfilled that church's wish list—and that is a typical written job description, by the way. To say yes would mean eventual death for most ministers in the congregation's eyes. Because no human being could achieve them, the pastor is in a you-lose position. Regardless of a minister's gifts, people skills, intelligence and experience, the performance expectations are often too high for anyone to succeed. And these are just the written expectations!

Maybe we shouldn't be surprised. The religious community killed Jesus because he didn't fulfill their expectations.

The Unwritten Rules

No relationship is a blank slate regarding expectations, verbal or invisible. We harbor expectations of the garbage man, the doctor, the taxi driver, the neighbor, and we certainly carry implicit expectations about the minister.

FACTS ON FILE

Expectations are the reason 33 percent of clergy leave their pastorate.[9]

Pastors "are one of the most frustrated occupational groups in our country. . . . The reason may have much to do with their inability to live up to the expectations placed upon them."[10]

One pastor laughed about expectations. "When Ken learned I drove 20 miles to get my hair cut (stopping to see shut-ins on the way), he began a whisper campaign and boycotted church."

Expectations find many ministers functioning as custodian, bus driver, sound technician, arbiter, gardener, referee, secretary and public relations expert. An urban pastor said, "In a given day, I might pull weeds and pick up trash in the church yard, mop the fellowship hall because the custodian didn't prepare it for a meeting, make coffee for a potluck, run copies for a special event, work with the tutoring program and sing with the music group."

FOR THE PASTOR
1. What hidden expectations have you encountered in your church?
2. How have you handled them?
3. At what point can you say to others, "This is who I am" regarding gifts and calling? And to yourself, "How badly do I need to be liked, to please people, here?"

Clergy are expected to counsel; shepherd; pray in public; evangelize; teach; preach; lead the youth; administrate and often run Christian education; make home, hospital, shut-in, emergency room and funeral visits; cater to the women's (and to some extent the men's) fellowship; oversee pledge and building campaigns; attend every event offered by the church; meet with every board or committee; and spearhead every movement and activity. In addition, they are expected to be the spiritual anchor at home, raise any children in the fear and admonition of the Lord, have a successful and loving marriage, and drive a decent car. It helps to dress nicely too. Whatever happened to focusing on the Word and sacraments?

Hazy job descriptions are part of the problem. In truth, many clergy feel like every member or attendee is a boss, each with specific job descriptions that are kept secret from the pastor. William Willimon writes:

> Most pastors work with ill-defined congregational expectations. They, therefore, feel as though they are always in a "no-win" situation. Expectations for their performance are so diverse and amorphous, related to each individual parishioner's vague picture of what a "good pastor" looks like, that the poor pastor never feels that he or she is doing the job. What is the job?[11]

No wonder pastors are exhausted, burned out and, in too many cases, leaving the ministry.

"One of the most discouraging aspects of pastoring is the extensive range of duties the pastor must fulfill," states George Barna. "We should initiate a major change in the status and expectations of the pastor by revising the job description."[12]

Show Your Hand

"Chest 'em," my grandmother would say when we played card games together. "Hold your cards to your chest so no one can see your hand." I have carried a "chest 'em" philosophy throughout life, whether it was cards or emotions or expectations. Only when I started realizing how this protective technique damaged relationships did I begin laying down my hand.

The church, too, "chests" its expectations of the pastor. Per-

---

FACTS ON FILE

"Four out of five adults say they expect the clergy to live up to higher standards than they expect of other people. Adults are pessimistic about the likelihood of the typical pastor meeting those standards."[13]

---

haps it is time to lay the cards on the table so everyone knows
what's in our hands. After all expectations are spread out, we
can evaluate what exactly we expect of the minister, what is
reasonable, and begin to negotiate. (For more on expectations,
see "Advice from the Pastor's Spouse" at <www.ivpress.com>.)

Acts and Expectations

The book of Acts provides an excellent example from the first
century of top priorities for a minister. In the early church,
complaints arose because widows were being overlooked in
food ministry. Seems as if the disciples were multi-tasking a bit
too much, even then.

> So the Twelve gathered all the disciples together and said, "It
> would not be right for us to neglect the ministry of the word of
> God in order to wait on tables. . . . Choose seven . . . from
> among you who are known to be full of the Spirit and wisdom.
> We will turn this responsibility over to them and will give our
> attention to prayer and the ministry of the word." (Acts 6:2-4)

Notice that prayer and ministry of the word are the most effective tools in ministry of any sort—and the first to be
dropped in many churches today because of pressing church
expectations and obligations. (For more on supporting your
pastor, see appendix A, "How to Pray for Your Pastor," and appendix B, "Bible Study on Loving Your Pastor.")

Other Scriptures to investigate when considering a job description and reasonable expectations include (discussions of
gifts in) Ephesians 4:11-12, (priorities in) 1 Timothy 4:13-14
and James 5:14. Freeing our ministers from extraneous expectations frees them to follow God's call and vision for their lives
and for the flock they sacrificially shepherd.

The church is in prime position to halt the steady decline
and demise of those in ministry. Setting guidelines in place for

adequate rest and renewal, we begin to contribute to the joy of their leadership (Heb 13:17) and the joy of their salvation (Ps 51:12). When our pastors are feasting on God's abundance, then we, the people, will be satisfied with the Lord's goodness.

Keeping the Pastor We Love

Do we make provision for our pastor's spiritual renewal (separate from vacation time)? How many hours a week does the pastor really work? Could we institute comp days?

Does the minister have a safe confidant? How can I contribute to the pastor's safety in our church?

What is our pastor's job description? Is it realistic? Does it match God-given gifts and abilities?

Is any dissatisfaction with the pastor a matter of unrealistic or unspoken expectations?

Since loneliness and isolation are factors in spiritual health, could I invite my pastor and family over and become family for the clergy?

Here is how I will pray for my minister:

5

Stress & Burnout

Come to me, all you who are weary and burdened,
and I will give you rest.

MATTHEW 11:28

T his is the most stressful time of my career," Quinn said in a phone interview. "I said yes to a church that was splitting down the middle. It's too much for me. And I have no one to talk to about it."

"Quinn, please get some help. You can't do this alone. Talk to another pastor, your superintendent, a counselor. Please."

"I can't. The competition, the boss, the town gossip. No one is safe. I have to hold it together myself."

Within weeks, word came back that Quinn died from a massive coronary. A wife and seven children mourned.

Stress and burnout have been called the twin destroyers of the pastorate. And with good reason.

Stress and Burnout Defined

Stress is continually demanding more of your body physically than it's designed for, pressing the body into emergency function with adrenaline demands, deadlines and commitments.

"Stress is the loss of fuel and energy which often produces panic, phobic, and anxiety-type disorders," says Dr. Archibald Hart.[1] Stress is rooted in the sense that there is never enough time, and pastors are particularly vulnerable to that gut-sick feeling. A minister's job is never finished. And stress is the number one contributor to the number one killer of our time—heart disease.

> "Stress? Stress is losing your husband all day until late at night. And then you lose him to 'relaxing' with a glass or two of wine or a few beers. Stress is seeing him go from crisis to crisis—ER to funeral home to volatile board meeting to terminally ill patient—and watching him become angrier and more run down. Stress is watching him consistently make choices that undermine his health, his marriage, his family and his faith. All for the church."
> *A clergy wife from Minnesota*

Primarily, stress is a biological response to the demands we place on our bodies. And our bodies raise a hue and cry. Cholesterol, blood pressure and heart rate all increase in times of stress, and the possibility looms large for ulcers, heart disease and nerve disorders.

A T-shirt at our local gym read, "Rest when you're dead." This belief system all too well describes how many pastors operate. Another T-shirt asked, "If you don't take care of your body, where will you live?" We need a new ministry motto: Rest and the pastorate cannot be mutually exclusive.

While stress is primarily a physical response, burnout, on the other hand, is largely an involuntary emotional response. It's a soul fatigue, accompanied by discouragement and demoralization. Burnout blurs the eyes like cataracts with the dual loss of vision and hope.

Burnout "often comes about when the victim has no adequate emotional support, no one to talk with when . . . isolated, alone, or even cut off from people who could help."[2] Where does the pastor go? Inward—thinking, "I must be strong. I must not share my problems with anyone." Research suggests that the root of burnout may actually be resentment.[3]

I asked Laura, a pastor from Arkansas, "What's one word to describe how you're feeling?"

Without pausing she said, "Depressed."

I was stunned. With her easy laugh and high enjoyment of life, depression didn't fit. "Why?"

"Not because of my work," she protested. "There's just not enough of me to go around. I'm too spread out." No, it's not about work—it is about not being two people!

The end result for both stress and burnout is depression.

At the close of an hour-long interview, I noticed an inconsistency between conversations with a family member and then with a former minister.

"Mike, I got the impression that your church chewed you up and spit you out," I said. "Why would your family member feel that way?"

This former minister laughed, then grew silent. Finally he answered, with spaces between each word, "Maybe because, for the last year of ministry, I lost thirty pounds, started seeing a psychiatrist and taking Prozac."

FOR THE PASTOR

"We need a new set of heroes among the clergy. We need persons who can make a church come alive without sacrificing their bodies, their families, or their souls."[4]

1. What kind of hero do you want to be?

2. Did you have superheroes in childhood?

3. How do you deal with the temptation to be one of those now?

4. How would you go about setting up parameters for this new type of heroism?

How can the congregation help reroute a pastor who is on the path of disaster and depression? Common denominators for stress and burnout are isolation and—surprise—expectations and spiritual drought. Peter talked about "administering God's grace in its various forms" (1 Pet 4:10). We can administer that grace by looking for practical ways to relieve stress and counteract burnout.

Pastors feel underappreciated, underaffirmed and overworked. In the words of a pastor from Illinois, "I'm more like a sprinkler than a hose. I'd rather be a hose." Another wrote, "I average a seventy-hour work week. The church does nothing to keep us from burning out. What really galls me is the carping and petty criticism from a few people who don't understand."

Support and Affirmation Are Not Luxuries

Pastors, spread too thin and too far for maximum effectiveness for the kingdom, risk losing their ministries, their faith and their joy. Most have experienced personal and professional crises that threatened to incapacitate their work.

For example, spiritual drought, isolation and unachievable expectations can destroy families. Over two years Dallas Theological Seminary professor Dr. Howard Hendricks collected 246 names of

---

DEFUSING THE TWIN DESTROYERS

■ Pray, pray, pray for your pastor and family. This is the front-line defense in waging war against the destroyer. (See the guidelines for prayer in appendix A.)

■ Exercise your spiritual gifts and responsibilities in the body of Christ. This takes the burden off the pastor of being "all things to all people."

■ Buy the clergy family a health club or YMCA membership. Pay for a racquetball court and meet the pastor there twice a week. Exercise relieves stress.

■ Fly the pastor to a conference on a topic he or she is passionate about, all expenses paid.

■ Encourage your pastor to find accountability and nourishment outside the church, and ask how you can help make room in the job for support.

■ Tell your pastor how a sermon changed your life.

■ Affirm the minister for character, not activity. For instance, "I admire your integrity in dealing with people," or "I see Jesus in you when I hear you interact with the elderly."

■ Don't count. Your shepherd's success is not based on numbers—how many converted, the number in the youth group—but on faithfulness and spiritual depth. Say this to the pastor!

ministers who confessed to moral failure. They had four common characteristics: they were not having personal time with God, were counseling the opposite sex, had no close friends and had the attitude, "It cannot happen to me."[5]

Stress and burnout both lead to isolation, creating an endless downward spiral.

Larris, a sixteen-year veteran pastor from Alabama, said, "My spiritual dryness is partly related to isolation. No one is safe as a confidant: not in my denomination, because the minister you choose may some day be your boss. And with jealousy between the local churches, I've chosen to go it alone."

This sense of isolation, this lack of mentors and of ministers' ministers surfaces repeatedly. Overwhelmingly, married pastors indicate that their spouses are their first choice for confidants. This not only increases the family pressure of ministry life, it creates a closed loop for outside objectivity and growth, placing additional strain on a clergy marriage.

Isolation weaves through stress and burnout like radioactive fiber. Support has demonstrable benefits. A nine-year study found that "people with many social ties (marriage, close friendships, extended families, church membership, or group associations) had a far lower mortality rate than those who lacked quality or depth in their social support systems."

Another study "indicated that men in their fifties, at high risk because of a very low social and economic status, but who score high on an index of social networks, lived far longer than high status men with low social network scores."[7]

FOR THE PASTOR
1. How frequently do you feel alone? Lonely?
2. Can you turn the aloneness into a spiritual discipline, a place of solitude where the goal is to seek God and let the aloneness transform you?
3. What is your risk factor when it comes to social ties and emotional/spiritual support systems?
4. If you could rank your stress level between one and ten, where would you land? Pay attention to physiological symptoms of stress as well. Take the burnout test in appendix E.

Pastors need to know that they are not alone in ministry—and that isolation is not God's plan. When Moses groaned before the Lord at the immense burden of carrying so many people, God responded by providing him seventy to share the load (see Num 11:14-17).

In "Working the Angles," Eugene Peterson writes:

> There is a saying among physicians that the doctor who is his own doctor has a fool for a doctor. If those entrusted with the care of the body cannot be trusted to look after their own bodies, far less can those entrusted with the care of souls look after their own souls, which are even more complex than bodies and have a correspondingly greater capacity for self-deceit.[8]

Ministers must have the church's blessing to pursue the support networks vital to their spiritual and emotional health. Like the rest of Christ's family, pastors cannot function well without practical friendships to weather the storms of life and the trials of ministry.

The effect on the local church, the impact on the community and the world will be dramatic when we begin to give double honor to our pastors (1 Tim 5:17). Whether an individual, a

Sunday school class or an elder board, all can follow Paul's plea to "refresh [the pastor's] heart in Christ" (Philem 20).

For true revival to break out in our churches and our world, we must begin to revive the shepherds. When we support and encourage our ministers through prayer, practical service and use of our gifts, we put power behind the prayer "Thy kingdom come."

Keeping the Pastor We Love

What signs of stress do I see in my minister?

In what practical ways can I share the burdens of ministry?

Does our pastor feel "underappreciated, underaffirmed and overworked"? How will I know?

What is our church's safety net for our minister? How often do we remind the congregation to pray for our pastor?

How can I encourage the minister toward rest, renewal and just plain fun, guilt-free?

Here is how I will pray for my minister:

6

Single Clergy

As she was preparing to move into her church community, lawn care and ladder work worried Emily. She asked the staff-relations committee for help in this area and then learned they had already made arrangements for her. Their thoughtfulness preceded her coming and has accompanied her throughout her pastorate. No more struggling with Christmas lights on eaves or cleaning gutters.

While 94 percent of ministers are married,[1] as a church we must also consider the single pastor. Needs, skills and time constraints vary. Single ministers caution against throwing them all in the same category; there are different types of singles. Said Janis, "Divorced or widowed clergy may miss being married, and so their needs and longings will be different than mine, since I have never been married." The single parent clergy, as well, can have different needs from others, especially by adding in parenting and custody dynamics. Emily's move to her parsonage along with her eighty-one-year-old mother created special needs; this will become increasingly common with the aging of America.

Expectations, a common area of conflict and misunderstanding, are no less an issue for single ministers.

Expectations

"People assume you're more flexible; being single doesn't mean we don't like stability," said Craig. "We're in the appointment system, and the cabinet typically gives me less transition time than they would a married pastor. I'm expected to pack up and move without the time for closure."

FOR THE PASTOR
1. What is your greatest job in ministry? Your greatest trial?
2. When have you felt expectations on you differed from those a married clergy might experience?
3. How do you interpret your needs and boundaries to your congregation? Where do you find a confidant/e in ministry?

Expectations extend to work hours as well. Churches tend to ask single clergy for more of their time, assuming they have more. "I'm spending the evening at home," is harder to understand than "I'm spending time with my family," said Vince. "When I go home after a long day or night of meetings, no one has done my laundry for me," said Janis.

And once at home, some people assume that single pastors can't cook, can't handle domestic tasks. "At age thirty," said Drew, "it's getting a little harder to laugh off." (For more on expectations see appendix B, "Bible Study on Loving Your Pastor.")

A common frustration for single clergy was the misunderstanding of relationships, whether self-care, friends, dating or extended family. "I have a home life," said Dave. "Though I live alone, I need space and time just like a pastor with a family. Parishioners don't always understand when they want me to work additional hours. And then I let 'family time'—home alone time—get eaten away with ministry. It's my fault too."

This plays out further in spiritual and emotional nurture for the single pastor: increased demands on time mean less focus on spiritual disciplines and life-sustaining relationships. One woman said, "Churches should put 'therapist' into their budget for clergy compensation." She laughed but made her point: isolation is an issue for the single as well as the married pastor. It's hard to sustain nurturing friendships, to find a safe place and a listening ear. "I pay a therapist; I'm under no illusion that she's a friend. But for one hour, I'm not taking care of anyone else, and I benefit from another's focused attention and wisdom."

The isolation may stem from others' discomfort with singleness. "When I first came to the church, they had a supper club. Only couples attended," Tom said. "That didn't fit very well for a single minister, and they began to realize how the supper club excluded people who didn't live in a couples world."

For Emily, invitations include her mother, and parishioners watch out for her when Emily is out of town. Their acceptance has created a social life for her mother as well as for Emily.

"The senior pastor and spouse tend to get more invitations to dinner or to another couple's home," said Brad. "And another couple would not typically invite me, a solo guy, out to socialize with them. People shy away from threesomes. But it doesn't have to be that way. Perhaps it's easier to invite a single clergy into a family setting."

This isolation intensifies noticeably during holidays.

I'll Be Home for . . .
"I'm at home this Christmas," said Karen. "I have no family in the

area and no plans for the holidays. It's awkward; I can't just ask if I can come over for dinner or to share the day with them. Then they feel obligated to invite me, and it's very stiff and unreal."

Brad agreed. "I'm in a small group of single pastors; none of us has family around, and we end up getting together for holidays. It's nice, but it's not the same."

The board or staff-parish committee can translate this awkward need to the congregation. Janis suggested an announcement by a board member: "This year our clergy will be in town for the holidays. Would anyone like to have them over to lunch?"

Dating

"Dating is very hard. Can you really date people in the congregation?" Drew asked. "It's also hard to find people who want to date a single pastor—the hours and schedule clergy keep are not attractive to the opposite sex. Plus we don't get weekends off; time is not my own."

"What are appropriate boundaries for the congregation? Asking about my dating life, matchmaking, trying to fix me up with a granddaughter . . . " Matthew shrugged. "It's hard to care without crossing the line and being invasive. It may also be hard for others to believe we can be happy as single people."

Karen said, "People assume that I date, but they also want me to be completely available to them. And they are curious but don't know how to ask."

What is the dividing line between friendly inquiry and invasive questioning? Your pastor is the only one who can answer that question.

Discrimination

When asked if they'd ever felt discriminated against because of their singleness, pastors unfortunately said yes in the areas of salary ("The married pastor before me had a larger compensation package"), job description ("I ended up helping the senior minister do all the stuff he didn't want to do") and expectations ("You can work more hours because you don't have a family to go home to").

The greatest gifts mentioned by single clergy were:

■ "My congregation is genuine. They expect that I have flaws. One of the best things congregations can do for pastors is to allow them to be on a journey themselves."

■ "My church is learning to expect me to have needs. They do not always enjoy hearing my needs and limits and boundaries, but I must tell them in order to not burn out, and to keep my sanity. They are very polite, respectful and loving in response."

■ "Keeping expectations in line with my spiritual gifts and my needs frees me to be all God has in mind. What a blessing."

Student loans are not lower for single graduate students. "I got out of school with a lot of debt, and with my compensation package I have almost nothing left over beyond basic living expenses. I have had to learn to live on a lot less," said Arleana.

"With the money I have left over to pay rent," said Janis, "I cannot afford to live near the church. And people in my congregation will take me out to show me some places I could afford, but those aren't safe. They wouldn't live there. So I am forced to commute an hour from affordable housing to my part-time pastoring job, and to my full-time job near the church which covers my benefits."

Regardless of marital status, a worker is still worthy of a life-sustaining wage.

Greatest Gifts

Even with these complexities, the pastors' reverence and strong sense of calling to ministry was very clear. "I am privileged to know my congregation intimately, to share their spiritual walks, to accompany them through the most joyous and the most painful moments of their lives. Feeling called by God to proclaim the Gospel and speak the truth," wrote one woman.

"I have no regrets about being ordained. It is very fulfilling and really what God intended for me. These struggles are difficult, but not impossible," said another pastor.

Congregation and pastor alike benefit when God calls single clergy into ministry. Learning to live together as the family of God, becoming extended family to the pastor and nurturing that person in ministry extend the welcome of Christ to the rest of world.

Keeping the Pastor We Love

What expectations do I have of my pastor, and how similar are those to my expectations either past or present of a married minister?

How does my church's compensation package for a single minister compare to that of married clergy?

In what ways can I reach out to my single pastor? What particular needs might I be able to meet?

Here's how I will pray for my minister:

THE SINGLE PASTOR

Dos
- Do reach out as couples, friends, family
- Do limit workweek expectations
- Do expect time for self-care, alone time, home time
- Do attribute domestic skills to single pastors
- Do accept the statement, "No, thanks, I need to be home tonight"
- Do assume other commitments in life: hobbies, interests, friends, activities, dating, extended family

Don'ts
- Don't assume loneliness
- Don't play matchmaker
- Don't put the pastor in a compromising position
- Don't reduce salary because of singleness (loans and mortgages are not lower due to single status)
- Don't forget to invite your minister over for meals or out for social time
- Don't assume flexibility

7

The Paragon
of the Pews

(or, How to Really Love
Your Pastor's Spouse)

*Let us consider how we may spur one another on
toward love and good deeds.*

HEBREWS 10:24

T he slim, vibrant woman moved through the pews. Eyes
alight with interest, she smiled, touched, laughed, compassion
evident. People responded with smiles, answering her questions with feeling, clearly pleased by her gracious attention.
After circulating, she headed for the front row, glancing around
for her children, who tore down the aisle to her side as the pre-
lude sounded. No one knew that her lovely suit came from a
resale shop for $3.50, that her children were dressed entirely in
hand-me-downs and that her heart was splintering.

No one warned her of how difficult ministry would be—how
hard it would be with her husband leading a flock of people
while she struggled with parenting dilemmas and went without
meat and milk to cut down on the food bill. Seminary profes-

sors had cautioned about the "other woman"—the church, the socially acceptable adulteress. She held everything together while he bottle-fed his ailing sheep. And she genuinely wanted to help her husband in ministry, which meant tying up the loose ends left from his too-many yes answers. For years she denied her primary gifts and calling because she was virtually a single parent. And now, seeking to use those gifts, her stress level escalated because she still bounced all the other responsibilities on her shoulders like so many fussy infants.

He was a wonderful father—when he was around. But that occurred so seldom that the baby cried when Daddy picked him up; he didn't recognize the man with the blond hair and sandy evening stubble. When the next child came to live unexpectedly in her womb, the slim, vibrant woman shed many tears until finally they began to ask the hard question, the question they vowed they would never ask: "Who will get the children?" She looked at ads for apartments, knowing that she wouldn't get the parsonage and that he would fight her for custody.

Meet the clergy spouse.

THE MOST WANTED LIST
(what your pastor's spouse needs from you)
■ Call the pastor at the office instead of home if possible.
■ Assume that you've hired and are paying only one minister, not the marriage partner.
■ Expect the same of the pastor's spouse as you do of any other member of the congregation.
■ Free clergy mates to use their gifts and talents.
■ Let them be human, and keep their confidences when they are.
■ Relay all messages, gripes and snipes directly to the pastor instead of the spouse.
■ Be realistic about clothing and standard of living, given the minister's salary.
■ Allow them to have a normal marriage, not a role-model marriage.
■ Let their actions speak for themselves and not for the spouse's ministry.

Where Seldom Is Heard an Encouraging Word . . .

They are everyone's friend but have few of their own. They always have an encouraging word, but scant are directed toward them. "Bear one another's burden" is their life motto. Though they listen intently, speak empathetically and love continually, ministry mates rarely receive the same in return. Benefits include numerous bosses, no written job description, no paycheck and often as many work hours as other professionals.

Pastors' spouses give at home, give at church and give up their marriages to ministry—and they are giving out. In one survey, 80 percent of clergy spouses struggled with depression.[1] Eighty-five percent of pastors spend two or less evenings home per week; 70 percent of pastors work more than sixty hours per week.[2] With these dynamics, clergy mates often feel like ministry widows and widowers. Adding to the strain, while bearing much of the burden of child rearing, homemaking and working, the spouse is also the minister's principal cheerleader and counselor. Further, the clergy mate carries much of the emotional and practical burden of making ends meet.

Though appearing to have it all together, the public face often masks private pain.

The triangle between minister, mate and congregation cannot be ignored. When their spouses are nurtured, shepherds are better able to tend their flocks.

Uniquely Positioned
The position of a pastor's marriage partner is unique compared to other professional couples, in or out of the church. Few other professions interview and examine the personal life, spir-

---

FACTS ON FILE

Burnout scores of clergy spouses may be as high or higher than the scores of paid contemporaries.[3]

---

ituality and giftedness of the spouse prior to hiring the job applicant.

Ministers' long work hours and on-call status compare to doctors'. But beyond a salary difference, doctors' spouses do not sit in on appointments, attend board meetings or watch through the surgery room window. Doctors' spouses are not expected to take an active interest in the doctors' work. They are certainly not expected to don scrubs and pick up a scalpel. Whether clergy partners desire it or not, expectations run high because of their high-profile marriages. This is especially true for women married to ministers. (Since approximately 5 to 7 percent of ministers are women,[4] research on their spouses is scant.)

Congregations want to be proud of their ministers' mates, introducing them as "my pastor's spouse." Parishioners regard them through slightly different lenses from other people in the pews. "Like it or not," says one clergy spouse, "this is not an ordinary layperson."

At a conference of ministry spouses, seventy-eight respondents to the question, "What is your greatest challenge in ministry leadership?" answered:

☐ loneliness and feelings of isolation
☐ balance of family and church
☐ expectations of church members
☐ criticism
☐ finances[5]

Noticeably absent in the responses was developing a deeper relationship with Christ. Only five stated their greatest challenge was "loving and pleasing Christ." Why might this be? Doctors deal with patients' "presenting problems"—the pain that gets them into the waiting room—and then look deeper for the core issue. The top five listed above are the presenting problems for spouses. Life in the ministry can be so over-whelming that the core, primary need for sustenance and fill-ing by God gets overlooked in the harum-scarum whirl. Surface pain hides the inner need, so we make our lists based on what we see.

The sense of exclusion from intimate relationships was widespread among female clergy spouses with whom I spoke, less so among men. We can't realistically expect the spouse to become everyone's best friend, but it helps to be aware of the loneliness factor.

More Expectations

Even holding the phone a foot away from her ear, the caller's voice carried perfectly to the clergy spouse. "Why weren't you at the parsonage when the people from the well company called?" Stan the church trustee shouted.

"What do you mean why wasn't I here?"

"They tried to call you yesterday. You should have been there!"

"Stan, we've waited ten days for their return call. I have a fam-ily and other commitments to tend besides sitting by the phone. We've had a contaminated well for weeks. Why did they wait so long to call?"

"That's not the problem. You should have been there." If Stan's reasoning weren't so infuriating it would have been funny. But neither of them was laughing.

FACTS ON FILE
Seventy-six percent of clergy spouses have felt lonely or out of place in the congregation.[6]

Weeks after the health department found fecal choliform in the parsonage well water, the unresolved problem required vigilance to prevent illness at home; her patience snapped at Stan's lack of understanding and care. "Stan, I'm not paid to be an operator at the parsonage. Maybe you'll want to hire someone to sit by the phone."

While this is an extreme (but true) example of misguided expectations and exasperation, the sense of being isolated and misunderstood as a result of those expectations seems universal for clergy spouses. In addition, the Alban Institute found that role expectations are the primary cause of their burnout.[7]

Before World War II, congregations considered clergy wives a "buy one, get one free" bargain. Not employed for pay, they were expected to embrace and reinforce the congregation's expectations, and accompany their pastor-husband in all forms of ministry. Now, from 50 to 70 percent of all pastors' spouses who are women work outside the home.[8] In spite of this, one survey found that 21 percent believe the congregation still views them as unpaid assistant ministers.[9]

FOR THE PASTOR AND SPOUSE

Many of us expect more of ourselves than is humanly possible—and more than God even expects of us. We strive for perfection based on our need to be needed, loved, affirmed and valuable, rather than finding those in the presence of God. We become like Adam and Eve, desiring to be like God, to take the place of God.
1. Where do you see this in yourselves, one another and your expectations?
2. How can you find more rest and less striving to meet others' expectations?
3. What did you expect out of ministry, and what did you get? How do you deal with the difference?

Whether expectations come from the minister, the spouse, the church, or even the previous clergy spouse, they are as potentially explosive as a mine field. Perhaps the best place to uncover leadership's expectations of the ministry spouse is through the staff-parish board, or elders, or even the women's or men's group. Itemizing group expectations and evaluating the list realistically are eye-openers. As a board, learning spouses' gifts and asking how they see themselves fitting in with the ministry of the local church facilitates openness and removes barriers to friendship. (For more on expectations, see "Advice from the Pastor's Spouse" at <www.ivpress.com>.)

Holy Human Syndrome

Parishioners may believe that their pastor's spouse stands a rung higher on the holiness ladder than laity. By virtue of ministers' calling, spouses are expected to be endowed with a higher degree of spiritual knowledge and giftedness. But Karla, a clergy mate in Illinois, says, "For years I wrestled with my position because I don't have Christian college or seminary training to be a Bible teacher. I couldn't step into the place of spiritual leadership people set aside for me, nor did I want to."

We cannot assume that all ministry spouses feel called to that position. Lydia, a committed spouse from Chicago, says, "Our church called my husband, not me. I want to be one of them, not set apart." Placing ministry partners on this pedestal leads to alienation and frustration.

Fortunately, the old taboo against clergy spouses having friends in the local congregation has lessened with time, especially as unchurched people enter the church. It seemed less

---

FACTS ON FILE

Fifty-three percent of ministers' spouses believed unrealistic expectations to be the biggest problem they face in the ministry they share with their pastor-spouses.[10]

---

critical with younger spouses and in larger churches. Taking clergy mates off the holiness ladder puts them on equal footing with others and lays to rest the specter of perfection. The church may lose a mythical holy human but gain a friend.

FOR THE PASTOR AND SPOUSE
1. What expectations do you have for one another when it comes to friends in the church? How do these show up?
2. In what ways might your spouse's close friendship with another in the church feel threatening or risky to you?
3. How do you think the church perceives friendships with you?

Gifts and Slot-Filling

Clearly, God brings together a variety of people with various giftings, which, when added together, equal a complete body, the church. Aware of our individual gifts and callings, we begin to prayerfully look for niches awaiting those precise gifts.

When we expect anyone, whether the pastor's spouse or the congregation's jack-of-all-trades, to fill the vacant or unpopular slots, we deny others the chance to say yes to God's gifts for that ministry. A common misunderstanding of the role of a clergy spouse is that if there is a hole to be filled, the spouse will bridge the chasm. (Harboring the same expectations of the pastor is uncommon.)

But that is unfair for all concerned. Saying yes unadvisedly means others cannot say yes deliberately. Some people have many gifts, others only a few, but it is a form of idolatry to expect slot-filling of anyone, even someone with a gift for helping.

Besides that, overworking one body part by expecting it to perform the functions of other parts means that the rest of the body atrophies. Unused muscles do not get stronger. Our expectations of others, whether the first couple of the church or laypeople, should be that all fulfill the unique calling God has for them.

Nearly every church we've entered has embraced me and allowed me the freedom to explore my gifts and calling, even to fail in the process. They have prayed for me and called me forward—and thus forwarded the work of God in this world in some small way through me. What a powerful influence the church can be!

Affirming Actions

Getting to know your pastor's spouse—passions, gifts, interests, character traits, experience, needs—is the first step toward affirmation.

When asked, "How has the church affirmed you as a clergy spouse?" Kevin answered, "Good question. They haven't, I guess. I'm greeted warmly when I'm at church gatherings. I get kudos when I teach adult Sunday school classes. They tell me how much they love my wife. But that's about it. I think that I'm a little scary to lots of people in the church, and they don't know what to do with me. Fortunately, I don't feel the need for affirmation from the congregation."

David agreed. "There's not much affirmation for men married to pastors." Laughing, he added, "I'm not too interested in joining the traditional group for spouses, which is the women's missionary society." And because of differences perceived be-

---

FACTS ON FILE

Only 51.7 percent of clergy spouses feel adequately trained for their role.[11] *Seventy-two percent struggle with depression.*[12]

---

tween male and female clergy spouses, he chooses not to partic-
ticipate in a clergy spouse support group.

Many pastors' spouses feel the church expects their involvement but leaves them out of the feedback loop after they've given
their time and talents. "Other members are thanked for their
work," said Natasha. "My contributions feel like part of the unwritten job description."

Scripture calls for the building up of the whole body of
Christ; the pastor's spouse is part of that body. Interviews suggest that husbands of clergy are even more likely to be left out
of "one another" care they deserve. Simple acts of appreciation
give a hefty boost.

FOR THE SPOUSE
1. What are the greatest gifts people in the congregation have given you?
2. Where do you find the greatest gaps in your life, whether emotionally, spiritually, financially, relationally?
3. What can you do about those gaps?

Deep Longings

Early in the pastorate I recognized a gnawing hunger for
accountability, spiritual depth and mentoring. I asked other
clergy spouses, "How do you stay alive spiritually?" Simplistic
answers ("Read a devotional every day") frustrated me and
increased my feelings of aloneness. Mentors topped my prayer
list, people who understood the ministry and could hold and
guide me to maturity.

FACTS ON FILE
*Fifty-five percent of clergy spouses felt they need help in
developing deeper relationships with God.*[13]

People in the church can rally here. Jesus discipled his followers; Timothy heard his pastor's heart when reading, "And
the things which you have heard from me in the presence of
many witnesses, these entrust to faithful men, who will be able
to teach others also" (2 Tim 2:2 NASB). Older women are to
teach the younger women (Tit 2:3-5). Whether your strength is
repairing automobiles, offering hospitality or leading Bible
studies, members of the congregation can tutor the clergy
mates from their own strengths. When mature believers open
their lives to clergy spouses, showing compassion and commitment to accountability and personal involvement, the entire
church benefits and grows.[14]

Random Acts of Kindness

How else can the church love practically? Spouses responded
with voices hushed by emotion, by disbelief, by humility.

"In the middle of a difficult pregnancy and a terrible transition, the doorbell rang," recalled one minister's wife. "The bike
shop owner held a new bicycle with a baby carrier attached. He
handed it to me, went back to his truck and pulled out a
matching bike for my husband, also with a baby seat. I burst
into tears."

"Sometimes, out of the blue, I receive a thank you note in
the mail expressing gratitude for my involvement," said another. "We paste these gifts into journals." Small stones of appreciation cast large circles.

Surprising acts of love are meaningful, regardless of cost. My
whole family jumped up and down for Karen's chocolate chip
banana bread. Norma, an avid couponer, frequently brought us
special cereal or another name brand deal. "It only cost five
cents," she demurred, but we felt honored and wrapped in fa-
milial love.

One of Leah's notes contained a list of dates and the message, "Please check your calendar. I'd like to care for Joshua so you can have a personal retreat monthly." Her generous gift allowed me to refill during a time when I was giving from a nearly empty well.

FOR THE PASTOR

1. In what ways can you encourage the congregation to affirm your spouse, without it sounding plaintive or selfish?
2. How do you feel when your spouse is encouraged? Ignored?
3. When have you come to your mate's defense because of the congregation's expectations?

Freedom and Friendship

By banishing the holy human specter, clarifying expectations and taking the initiative in affirming and reaching out to pastors' spouses, a quiet revolution may occur in the pews and at potlucks. By encouraging them like any other members of the body of Christ, they are better able to follow God's calling on their lives, and to fortify their spouses for ministry. The result will be healthier leaders, happier congregations and warm friendships, which in turn warm the world.

Keeping the Pastor—and Spouse—We Love

When do I or others place the clergy spouse on a pedestal?

How can I connect with my pastor's spouse?

Where have I seen the slot-filling expectation? What can I do to fulfill my own gifts and calling in my church, and thus be faithful?

Putting aside false humility, where would I feel competent to mentor the clergy spouse? Where do the spouse's needs and my gifts or strengths meet?

What expectations do I harbor toward the ministry mate? Are they realistic? Harmful?

How well do I know my minister's spouse—gifts, needs, dreams, history?

Here's how I will pray for my pastor's spouse:

8

Creating a Place
for the Children

But Jesus said unto them, Suffer the little children to come unto me, and forbid
them not: for of such is the kingdom of God.

MARK 10:14 (KJV)

Perched on the kitchen stool holding a pink envelope, I felt
my children's world tilt and teeter on the axis of someone else's
expectations. Five pages, hand printed and single-spaced, detailed
my problems as a parent and my son's as a five-year-old. The section that was outlined, underlined and indented incensed me.

☐ He should be an example to others reflecting Christian exam-
ples—not a terror or classroom/parish kindergarten bully. . . .
☐ His behavior and how you deal with his problems not only
reflect on [your son] but upon you and your husband, very
much. Maybe you need to read, pray and reflect on what the
Bible says of a minister and his family. . . .
☐ . . . You'll lose the trust and welcome of your parish and over-
all community.

Though sounding like some obscure code of conduct for the
vicar's children from the 1800s, this letter concisely summed

up the dilemma of the pastor's family. Children must exemplify Christian virtue, regardless of their ages. Their behavior reflects positively or negatively on the pastor as parent and "professional" Christian; job security and community respect hinge on the children's actions.

A Reality Check

Giggling teenagers talked with animation. "Wouldn't it be great to be in Pastor Dan's family?" "He is so cool." "It must be wonderful."

For most pastors' kids (PKs), the pastorate is not always heaven on earth, nor one great youth group experience full of campfire songs and ice-breaker games. The only perfect Parent had only one perfect Child. The rest of us blow it frequently. Pastoral families face the same problems, pressures and perplexities as other families, with added difficulties unique to ministry.

Job Security

One difference shows up in clergy job security. The CEO's kid is hardly expected to display advanced management knowledge at age five; the shop owner would not lose customers should her kindergartner pull another child's hair; the electrician wouldn't be fired for an offspring's misbehavior. The garbage man would not be put on notice because his teenager's room looked like a salvage yard.

FACTS ON FILE

Forty-nine percent of pastors say "Pastoring this church has been difficult on my family."[1]

Yet PKs may wonder, "Will my parent lose this church if I'm not perfect?" One minister said, "They judge my credibility by how well I take care of my wife and kids. And that is close to Scripture. But I'm also expected to work every waking hour." Can we determine pastoral effectiveness without also considering preaching, pastoral care and leadership?

FOR THE PASTOR AND FAMILY
1. Have your children wondered if your job was at risk because of their actions? How have you handled this?
2. How attached are each of you to the other's reputation? That is, if another misbehaves in public, how do you feel?
3. When have church members loved and affirmed you? Could you write family notes telling how they have impacted your life, your family and the kingdom?

Boundaries

Boundaries mean that you do not have to be who I think you should be. You are not me, and I am not you. Inappropriate boundaries make it easy to blame others because they don't measure up, but the problem is in not respecting differences between us. This respect is crucial to children's developmental process.

Typically, a boundary separates the parent's job from the

FACTS ON FILE

"Eighty percent of practicing pastors think ministry negatively affects them or their families."[2]

"Most pastors work in excess of 70 hours a week. Seventy percent don't take a week of vacation during the year, and 60 percent don't get a full day off during the week."[3]

---

child's behavior—except for pastors, who are naturally expected to live out the principles they embrace, and their children, who are often expected to exemplify those principles regardless of age. Ministers' jobs become inseparable from family identity.

Clergy kids may not know that age-inappropriate expectations violate boundaries, as do rules about their parents' jobs. These violations deny those children the chance to find their special, God-given identity. They also heap on deadly shame, that sense of being a failure, never able to measure up, never good enough.

None of us, frankly, are good enough. That is why we need a Savior. And as we move closer to our Savior, and further away from expecting midget messiahs in pastors' children, we will begin to truly become the family of God for them.[4] In the pastorate, boundaries easily blur because of subtle and not-so-subtle expectations.

Much work and ministry occur at home, confusing normal work and family distinctions. The home phone number on church letterhead and the Sunday bulletin gives people blanket permission to call the home—and for the pastor and family to forget that home is separate from work. Dynamics are set, then, for omnipresent expectations by

---

CONGREGATIONAL CRIB SHEET: REINFORCING NATURAL BOUNDARIES

■ Give credit for making good choices and for doing things well, rather than saying, "They're the minister's kids. Of course they memorized the verses." They are not extensions of the pastor or mini-ministers.

■ Separate their actions from the parent's job. PKs misbehave in relative proportion to the rest of society's children, church members' included.

■ Get to know them as individuals: their likes, thoughts, gifts.

■ Allow the clergy family to determine the extent of the family's involvement in church, just as any other member would do.

■ Make phone calls to the pastoral home only in emergency, honoring the work and home separation. Remember, their parent is the PKs' minister as well; children must be considered part of the flock.

the people for the pastor and for omnipotent need-meeting by the pastor—even if it disrupts sacred family time.

FOR THE PASTOR

1. How well do you separate work from home? What does your family think?
2. How do your work habits contribute to the expectations of omnipresence and omnipotence?
3. How many evenings are you gone each week? What does your family think about this? How did you envision parenting in terms of your commitment, availability and the pastorate?
4. How can you add family space to your schedule? How can your kids?

One minister's daughter wrote, "My dad was never on time for dinner, if he ever made it home at all before I went to bed." A son said, "My dad threw the ball with me one time in my life. He was gone a lot."

This is a unanimous regret for clergy. One minister said, "In the time demands that the church and I placed on myself, I was seldom around in the evenings. I confused loyalty to God with loyalty to my job, and forgot that my loyalty to God placed my spouse and the family ahead of my job as a pastor."

Expectations

In the pastorate, home offers no family protection from the expectations of the "boss," the church. Work is always there, linking children with expectations of spiritual maturity. The most common disadvantage for PKs surveyed was, as a twelve-year-old stated, "More people expect you to be Christian-like all the time. It is impossible to be perfect."

PKs are not saints by virtue of family arrangement; these children did not choose their parents' profession. No one is born with a full-fledged, fruit-bearing faith, even kids in pastors' homes. (For more on expectations for PKs, see the section "What About Preachers' Kids?" at <www.ivpress.com>.)

Relatively Speaking

"Several members go out of their way to show our children they are valuable human beings on their own," wrote a stay-at-home dad and clergy spouse. "Some attend their performances, others give them gifts, others pray for a specific child. As a minister's family, we are sometimes aware of how many people pray for us individually and as a group."

One dad, whose wife is an associate pastor in a suburb, said, "The kids were immediately accepted in church. They were treated as though special, quickly developing great friendships." The instant social setup made for an easier move.

God's people can play huge roles in the lives of pastoral children, sowing blessing and affirmation and deep faith by their presence and prayers.

In our transient society, separation from extended family is inevitable for many. The pastor's family is no different, but geographical and social restraints may isolate them even more from family-type experiences.

"Mom," a child asked before the Christmas program, "why don't *our* relatives ever come see us in school plays?"

A hand of sorrow squeezed my heart. The children noticed

PKS' ADVICE ABOUT HOW TO TREAT THEM

■ Don't try to pump them for information you know is none of your business anyway. Linda, 50

■ Treat them like any other kid. Debbie, 11

■ Welcome them, make them feel at home, be their friend. Ben, 15

■ You don't have to remind us of our responsibility. Believe it or not, we hear it at home. Give us some grace? Just *show us* an example. We'll turn out okay. Timothy, 14

■ Treat them like any other kid; they're no different, they have the same pressures of sex, drugs, and some get into it because of all the pressure they feel from parents and church. Mainly from church people. Courtney, 14

■ I think that a church can be supportive of their pastor's family without holding them at an arm's length. We aren't religious fanatics and it's even been told that we make pretty good friends. Heather, 19

■ Treat us with respect. We deserve it. Erika, 14

■ Include them in outings with your own children, especially to places they might not be able to afford. Rachel, 28 grandmas and grandpas snapping pictures, holding video cameras. Kids don't notice how many children *don't* have family present; they just want the delicious joy of saying, "Watch me!" with doting, caring people available for the job.

When our schedule began to feel like a ride on the Tilt-a-Whirl, with cars breaking down, hockey games and dual ministries conflicting, we called, "Help!" For four years Ray and Norma had our kids for occasional overnights, loaded Christmas stockings, gathered school supplies in August and filled baskets in spring. They shuttled to ballet and the YMCA, helped when I had surgery, took a kid or two to the fair. One of their gifts to the church, they felt, was caring for our children. We were humbled, helped and blessed.

With Ray and Norma, our kids experienced total presence and life-giving attention from grandparent-like adults, and they came home filled to the brim with good food, good memories and love. "Love," writes Dean Merrill, "is giving someone your undivided attention."[5]

This model for family began at Calvary. Throughout his earthly ministry, Jesus seemed to be redefining relationships. Some of his last words on the cross point us toward a new understanding of family. "Dear woman, here is your son," Jesus said to his

---

FACTS ON FILE

Eighty-five percent of pastors spend two or less evenings per week at home.[6] *Such involvements may be part of the written or unwritten job description.*

Ninety-four percent of pastors feel pressure to have "an ideal family." Sixty-one percent of pastors indicated their children felt pressure "in being the child of a minister."[7]

---

mother as she grieved at his feet. "And to the disciple, 'Here is your mother.' From that time on, this disciple took her into his home" (Jn 19:26-27).

When we see our pastors' kids through the eyes of Christ, our expectations will not hinder them. In a very real sense, the church is a proving ground for PKs' identity and faith: if Christ is authentic, if this Christianity stuff is valid, God will show up in people's lives. Modeling integrity, discernment and joy, getting to know the people in the pastorate, and giving of ourselves in small and big ways will bring the greatest reality check of all: that Jesus is alive and well, and living in and through the church.

And we will let the children come.

Keeping the Pastor We Love

How do I help the pastor to be above reproach (Tit 1:6)?

What expectations do I have of the pastor's children? How does this compare with biblical standards? With age-appropriate standards?

How do my expectations of the pastor—omnipresent, omnipotent—harm the pastor? The children?

Write a sample of what a Bill of Rights for PKs and their families might look like.

How can I communicate acceptance and grace to the family?

Here is how I will pray for my pastor's children:

9

Ministry & Church Accountability

Iron sharpens iron, so one [friend] sharpens another."
PROVERBS 27:17 (NASB)

Mrs. Rubietta, I'm a safe," my daughter's friend said to me one evening when we were all hanging out in our kitchen. I looked at her, trying to figure out how that worked. My daughter bailed me out of my ignorance and lack of imagination: "She locks up everything she hears. Any secret is safe with her. She's a safe."

We need more safes in our lives and in our churches: people who have proven compassion and an interest in our lives, who can listen deeply, care and hold confidences.

To be a safe, we prove to be life-giving with our words and friendship. "Death and life are in the power of the tongue" (Prov 18:21 NASB). A loose tongue can destroy an entire ministry and family and church and generations of people—which means those in positions of responsibility don't blab all their inner feelings and anguish. So don't feel badly if you aren't the safe for your pastor. But pastors and ministry couples need a safe, somewhere.

How can we support our pastors and help them to find accountability in the most important parts of life?

Intimacy and the Pastor

Ministers are not exempt from the troubles and temptations luring parishioners or anyone else. Further, pastors' marriages are equally susceptible to busyness, crisis, poor communication, fighting, money mismanagement, addiction, adultery and plain old lack of interest. Heavy expectations leave little energy to breathe life into tired relationships.

Because the ministry marriage is expected by many to be an example of perfect romance and faithfulness, it may be difficult for pastors to acknowledge marital problems or to consider building blocks in marriage. Couples need thawing time to shift out of work-perform-produce mode and into relationship. Building blocks include basic things like communication, shared interests, exercise and just plain play. Major things like forgiveness and repentance and a mutual spiritual journey—these bring life to every marriage, pastors' included.

With forty years' experience as a pastor's wife, Gail Mac-Donald, in *High Call, High Privilege,* states several themes that have helped to preserve and enhance her marriage to Gordon.

"Mutual time at the fire" (intimate connection with God as a couple: developing spiritual depth together, praying together, reading deeply and devotionally).

"Time to live" (dating, having "surprise nights," playtime).

FACTS ON FILE

Eighty percent of clergy and 84 percent of their spouses are either discouraged or struggling with depression.[1]

"Time to talk" (cultivating both the desire and the ability to talk with one another).

"Marital quiet time" (time for husband and wife to catch up on the day, every day, alone).

"Time under control" (taming the calendar and demands on life, before they drain the life out of the marriage).

"Time to deal with your weakness" (facing up to "weaknesses, character flaws and failures").[2]

Gail comments, "I'm prepared to call these principles non-negotiable. That is: You probably can't have a healthy marriage in a congregational setting without them. They won't guarantee a fail-safe marriage, but they can serve to diminish the possibility of a relationship headed for mortal damage."

These are the areas that elders, church boards and pastoral care committees will want to talk about with the pastor. Questioning ministers about their marriages may feel like meddling to both parties! It's important to make clear to your pastor that asking about their marriage doesn't mean you think the marriage is on rocky turf. And it will be the role of only a few to ask the hard questions. (For more ways to build up your minister's marriage, see "Building up Your Pastor's Marriage" at <www.ivpress.com>.)

Accountability

One speaker reportedly asks men when meeting them, "Are you being faithful to your wife?" He doesn't assume involvement in adultery or pornography or workaholic unfaithfulness, but he knows the value of accountability. Many gasp at the audacity—who asks anyone this question, or any politically incorrect ones? But why not? All people, including the pastor, need others in their lives to ask the hard questions.

Let's say you notice the minister at church late night after night and early morning after morning for meetings and Bible studies. You might ask, "Say, Pastor, you're at church so often lately. Must be hard on you and your spouse. How's it going at home?"

FOR THE PASTOR
1. Who asks you questions about your inner life? Your marriage?
2. Whom do you invite into your heart to hold you before God for the very best in your marriage and ministry?

The pastor's first response: "Fine. Great." Denial is a handy tool, designed to get people through a difficult time until they can emotionally and spiritually and even physically do the work necessary for healing. You nod, smile, appreciate the answer, then ask, "How often do you two get away on an overnight? Or even a date?"

Possibly the pastor's mind will be filling with excuses and even defensiveness. "Well, I have all these meetings. We both work too late. The kids need so much attention. We're too tired. We have no money."

You say, "Tell me about your dreams for your marriage. Maybe we can figure something out . . ." Sound simplistic? Maybe. But we have to start somewhere.We must be willing, either as a friend, board-appointed elder/overseer or liaison, to compassionately come alongside the pastor. "Your marriage relationship

---

FACTS ON FILE

The average clergy "ever-divorced" rate (24% of women and 19% of men) is similar to the total lay "ever-divorced" rate most recently reported by the Census.[3]

A primary cause for a high ministry drop-out rate for at least one mainline denomination is the spouse's discontent.[4]

---

is more important than your work in this church. We support
you in building up your marriage and want to pray for you,
help you. How can we do that?" For single clergy, ask how to
pray for them and hold them accountable to living above
reproach.

One minister with excellent counseling skill was impervious
to his wife's pleading for marriage
counseling. "There is nothing they
can tell me, frankly." Not only is
this arrogant, it overlooks the obvious: one person cannot corner
the market on any type of knowledge, and one person cannot be
God (as hard as we often try). An
emotionally objective third party
can defuse denial and defensiveness, and remove barricades of resentment. This minister agreed to
counseling only when the elder
board said to him, "You have no
understanding of how your actions affect other people. We
strongly urge you to get counsel-
ing and will hold you accountable for that." The spouse believes that the board's intervention and the ensuing counseling
saved his ministry and their marriage.

WATCH OUT! ACHTUNG!
DANGEROUS INGREDIENTS FOR
MINISTRY
■ Excessive night meetings
■ High fatigue
■ Continual crisis mode at church
■ Friction between church staff
■ Staff turnover or addition
■ Heavy counseling load—
especially with the opposite sex
■ Financial strain on the pastor
■ Crisis or change at home—new
baby, health, problems with
children, a special needs child,
change in spouse's work, in-law
care
■ Heavy travel schedule for
pastor or spouse
■ New program at church: pledge
drive, fund-raising, building
program

Preventing Clergy Catastrophe

Accountability could help prevent a primary cause of clergy
catastrophe: sexual temptation. In March of 2001, Focus on the
Family's Pastoral Ministry department received 483 crisis calls
from forty-seven states in the United States and most of the

provinces of Canada. The top two problems concerned sexual issues and marital problems.[5] How does this happen? How can we prevent this?

Meeting in an open area with a third person around or insisting on working as a trio on a project keeps the temptation down. Working closely with a lay leader or support staff of the opposite sex for an extended period of time in an isolated setting can be dangerous. We are not looking for tarantulas under every rock or the devil around every corner—nor are we being alarmists to take these precautions. Very few begin a working relationship with the intention of committing adultery—whether emotionally or physically. Besides, why give the enemy an opportunity to attack?

FOR THE PASTOR

1. When have you experienced the seduction of emotional intimacy with another—and how have you combated it?
2. What precautions do you take to prohibit opportunities for inappropriate intimacy?
3. How do you keep your thoughts pure?
4. What is your reaction to the possibilities of stumbling in this way? "No way"? Please do not let pride stop you from being cautious. You are worth protecting.

The classic case of moral failure in the ministry is the pastor who crosses the boundaries of propriety with a counselee because of the emotional intensity of the counseling problems. In counseling, due to sharing personal details and pain, the counselee plunges fast-forward into emotional intimacy, perceiving the pastor as gentle, wise, caring, spiritual and attentive. Because no one else acts in this manner, affection is transferred to the pastor. The pastor in turns feels good about being so needed and helpful, and is sucked into deeper intimacy against all common sense. This show is rerun daily in churches across

North America. The church can help by setting appropriate guidelines for counseling situations in particular.

Some pastors insist on an office door with a window, so they are visible. Others leave the door open several inches. Church boards may set a maximum number of times for a pastor to counsel someone, perhaps three. Billy Graham believes his policy of never being alone with a woman has kept him above reproach. Many pastors counsel alone only with couples, or have a safe third party present when counseling the opposite sex. Some boards require that a pastor be accompanied by an elder or another person when making house calls.

Another, less visible area of sexual temptation is pornography. Dr. Archibald Hart ranks it as the top problem for pastors today.[6] Anonymous and increasingly accessible, thanks to the Internet, pornography is a hidden addiction with far-reaching consequences for a pastor's personal life as well as family and church. How can a church guard against the dangers of pornography for the body of Christ, which includes the pastor? Research the dangers, then present the findings and strategies for combating this accessible evil. Preach it from the pulpit. Offer a Sunday school or adult education class; start a support group for people struggling with the problem.

If you suspect your pastor struggles in this area, insist on an accountability colleague and counseling. Instrumental in beginning recovery groups in the church, Rev. Ted Roberts suggests it may take four years of all-out fighting to beat this insidious addiction.[7]

To truly honor pastors, someone must ask discerning questions about their thought life, where they struggle with sin, where they are most easily tempted. Asking pastors how this line of questioning and accountability would look for them personally is appropriate.

With relationships in general in disrepair, honoring your pastor through gentle accountability will build up the church as well, creating an atmosphere of support, encouragement and honesty. Because relationships are made in heaven. And so are ministers. Single or married, we need to build them up on earth.

SUGGESTIONS AND GUIDELINES FOR ACCOUNTABILITY

As an elder board or staff-parish board, determine how to hold the pastor accountable for healthy boundaries at work so the pastor's personal life and marriage flourish.

■ Determine how many night meetings are essential.

■ Limit the pastor's job description so it can fit into a normal work week.

■ Ask the pastor to help set appropriate ways to be held accountable, without it seeming like meddling to anyone concerned.

■ Ask the minister to write out a personal relationship mission statement that includes top relationships: God, self, spouse, children.

■ Then invite the minister to flesh out tangible goals for those relationships, goals that express scriptural values, such as three nights at home, one inviolable date each week, two weekends away each year. Commitments in the marriage to spiritual depth, communication, play and practical help should show up in those goals.

■ Determine how the pastor should proceed safely with a counseling ministry, since this is an area of both temptation and stumbling, and can do permanent damage to many people.

■ If the pastor is offended or not willing to be held accountable for appropriate boundaries, suggest outside counseling or require it. Leaders must be willing to answer to others for their lives and their impact on people, including spouses and family.

■ Regarding sexual temptation: the accountability person must dare to ask tough questions with gentleness and not judgment.

Keeping the Pastor We Love

What expectations do I have of my pastor's marriage? How realistic are those expectations given the demands on time and energy we also have of the minister?

How can I be a "safe" for the pastor/couple?

Is there a couples' study we could do to get to know one another?

What accountability structure is in place for my minister? Are there guidelines for counseling and working relationships?

Here's how I will pray for my pastor (and spouse):

10

Hearth & Home

*I will make My dwelling among you. . . . I will also walk among you and be
your God, and you shall be My people.*

LEVITICUS 26:11-12 (NASB)

Rich and Jane, meet Harion. He's drawing up the blueprint
for your new parsonage." We gaped at the man with this rare
mission. Neither of us had ever lived in a new home (nor have
we since!), and our experience of parsonages consisted of a
spacious, hundred-year-old farmhouse with green stuff growing on basement walls.

"When can we get together to go over ideas?" Harion asked.

Had I remembered to close my mouth at first, it would have
popped open again like a spring-loaded gate. They wanted our
ideas? They cared what we thought and needed? We would
help design this house? Down to the home office with an outside entrance and a half-bath (so meetings could be held
there—in the office, not in the bathroom!—and people
wouldn't have to tromp through our home and disrupt family
life should nature call during a gathering), choice of carpeting,

wood stain, flooring, paint and even wallpaper.

First Thessalonians 5:12-13 (NASB) says, "We request . . . that you appreciate those who diligently labor among you, . . . and that you esteem them very highly in love because of their work." This reminds me of that church. Other places also come to mind, but this was the most incredible generosity we'd witnessed to date when it came to honoring the pastoral family. Here the storehouses of heaven spilled over. The effect of being cherished made those powerful ministry years. That home hosted so many people, meetings, children, play dates, counseling sessions, support groups and just plain living—good thing they installed sturdy carpet! Further, the church's love and attention to our needs set us free to love and care for others.

Parsonage Living

Call it a manse, vicarage or parsonage, there are advantages— and some disadvantages—for the inhabiting pastor. Statistics are difficult to track down. One researcher found that 58 percent of pastoral couples live in church-owned homes, meaning that 42 percent own or rent their homes. Of the 58 percent, half would like to own their own home.[1] According to the results of Census 2000, 67.4 percent of adults live in owner-occupied housing.

Proximity to church is a prime advantage—work is an easy commute and saves wear and tear on the wheels! The pastor can run home for a meal, a bedtime story and an emergency too. Once our toaster caught fire, and our older kids raced to church shouting, "Dad, Dad, the kitchen is burning!" He has never made the trip in so few seconds!

Our sociable children loved visiting with people coming into the church via the sidewalks or parking lot, which usually bordered the parsonage yard. One summer, our kindergartner graciously hosted impromptu snack-fests with exchange students from Spain. The location of the parsonage works well when the kids want to have sidewalk stands too—one family entrepreneur had quite a business selling rocks once.

FOR THE PASTOR
1. What preference do you have for parsonage versus home ownership? Why?
2. How does this match your current arrangement?
3. What needs do you need to communicate to your people?
4. What steps can you take to feel better about current living arrangements?

In some areas, parsonages are furnished (this can be a disadvantage, since furnishings may be church castoffs or rummage sale leftovers). This reduces some moving headaches and lowers the cost of a move for the church and the pastor. Also, with a church-owned home, there are no selling/buying problems for the pastor.

Every house is a fixer-upper, regardless of age. In a parsonage, repairs and maintenance, the downside of home owning, become church budget expenses and not the pastor's, as do improvements. This is a real pastoral perk.

Advantages of a Parsonage for the Church

After it's paid for, a parsonage frees up the budget so only maintenance and improvements are necessary.

Proximity is another advantage; most parsonages are close to the church, and with the minister literally a stone's throw away, accessibility is never a problem.

There is stability for the church in knowing where the pastor will live.

A parsonage is a good investment for a church since property values generally rise.

Church property tends to be well situated for resale should it be necessary.

Many churches prefer that the pastor live in the neighborhood of the church; a parsonage guarantees this.

Disadvantages of a Parsonage for the Pastor

The obvious disadvantage to parsonages is that they simply may not fit the pastor-family's needs.

Proximity to church is also a disadvantage. Transients frequently visited our homes, somehow knowing a pastor lived there. I felt vulnerable at these times with small children and a husband working long hours away from the house. One church sponsored a homeless shelter during the cold months, and our driveway was also the church parking lot where they gathered in the night to smoke and so on. We had many wonderful interactions with the guests and several frightening incidents. It was not always safe to let the children play; but conversely, our children grew to understand many of their own blessings and responsibilities when interacting with the guests.

The parsonage yard frequently adjoins the church. For one pastor, staff offices overlooked the family's play yard and back deck. The minister never felt comfortable playing catch in the yard, relaxing for a few minutes off or cooking out on the deck because of observation from church windows. Having people constantly aware of one's activities and leisure makes it hard to punch off the clock.

I tried—with limited success—to regard the high visibility of our home and family as an opportunity to live like Christ in the parsonage, believing that those who maintained a strong awareness of our activities could also be considered the "great cloud of witnesses."

The issue of boundaries returns in any discussion of a parsonage. Boundaries are difficult for both church and pastor to remember. Some pastors recall people just walking into their home without knocking, figuring that since the church owned it, members deserved unlimited access. Some clergy have been told by church members, "We're paying your electric bill—why do you use so many lights?"

Church overflow and meetings may habitually get shoved to the parsonage. "Can't you have the Sunday school in your living room?" "We'll use the parsonage for Monday night meetings." "You'll have to clear everything out of the kitchen. We always use it to cook for our fundraising dinner." "The youth group always meets at the parsonage." These are all comments heard in years of parsonage living.

The parsonage is a separate home for the pastor and is part of the pastor's ministry only as deemed appropriate by the family, not by the church.

Having others in charge of the cost of home maintenance and repairs is a blessing; it may also result in neglect. Because the church doesn't live in the home with the problem, repairs may be put off or discounted, to the discouragement, inconvenience and devaluation of the pastor. One pastor with good fix-it skills could never get the board to remedy problems. He spent his time and money without reimbursement to keep the home livable.

Most disadvantages to parsonage living are more inconvenient than insurmountable. Possibly the biggest pitfall for pastors is equity—where will they go when they retire? According to the IRS,[2] a church-owned home is seen as part of a minister's "income," and the fair rental value (cost of rent plus utilities for a similar-sized rental home in the community) is the basis of the higher social security taxes ministers pay.

But should pastors leave the ministry or retire, they end up without a home in spite of all the years they paid social security taxes for the temporary benefit. Should the pastor die, the family in the parsonage is truly homeless. For all practical purpos-

---

MAKE THE PARSONAGE A HOME
- Set up a refurbishing account; create a line item in the budget.
- Establish minimum standards for the parsonage (see appendix F, "Housing Help: Sample Parsonage Guidelines").
- Appoint a liaison with a heart for the home and the pastoral family to keep tabs on needs, suitability, repairs. This prevents the pastor's family from feeling like beggars when problems arise.
- Create a policy on repairs. Include timeliness of the repair after the problem/ need arises and who calls the repairperson.
- Inspect the home for needs and potential problems annually; give the family adequate warning, and accommodate their schedule.
- Make sure it fits their space requirements. If the family outgrows the current home, what backup plans exist?
- Will the yard suit family needs? Small children may need a fence or a lock on the gate.
- Is the home hospitality-ready? Would you want to entertain guests there?
- Is the parsonage on a par with the homes in your congregation?
- The parsonage represents your level of respect for your pastoral family and their value to you, as well as your acceptance of their humanity. How much do you care?

---

es, pastors in parsonages do just as lifelong renters do—throw money away. For good stewardship on the minister's part, owning makes more sense.

Disadvantages of the Parsonage System for the Church
What if it doesn't suit the pastor in some major way? What alternatives are possible? Might the right minister refuse a call because the parsonage is ill suited?

Parsonage inspection, upkeep and improvement are necessary and inconvenient.

Moving from a housing allowance to a parsonage requires church capital for the down payment.

Increasingly, ministers desire home ownership, leaving the

church saddled with both parsonage and housing allowance, at least during that particular pastor's stay.

Home Ownership

The pastor's family lined the front pew. The all-church meeting to decide whether to change from the parsonage system and allow the pastor to purchase a home generated heated discussion among congregants. Acutely uncomfortable as their finances and future was questioned, the pastoral couple wondered if the process was worth the embarrassment and discomfiture. After two decades in ministry, with children from high school to grade school, they had never owned a home. The typical family at the meeting not only owned a home, their income doubled the clergy family's.

Arguments ebbed and flowed. Finally, a member, a pastor's daughter, stood. "My parents never had a home in all their years of ministry. Now near retirement, they have only just been able to start plans for a place to live when Dad leaves ministry. They've given their best years for God's work, and the church never thought to provide them with a means of building equity for retirement. I don't want that to happen to my pastor's family. I move that we change to a housing allowance and let the pastor have a home. Now, while they can still build some equity for retirement."

"Most Americans dream of owning a home," said one man. "Every person needs a place to call his or her own, a place where they are off duty. Why should a minister be any different?"

After more discussion, the leader called for a vote. The pastoral family left the room and paced off the wait in the minister's office. Air barely squeezed past the tension in their throats. Here are the clergy spouse's words:

How horrible to hear debate about why the church should or shouldn't use the parsonage for needed space and programs, and provide us a housing allowance of similar value. How humiliating. Still, I hope I never forget the sea of supportive people crowding the room. . . . Oh, God, to see our kids' faces and know the joy they felt at the positive outcome. To see my husband respond with lighthearted laughter for the first time in months, to see his sense of affirmation and belonging, and a new feeling that he could stay and minister in this place. . . . I have never felt so loved.

That vote marked a turnaround in the pastor's morale and his sense of being valued in his role in that church and as a human being with normal needs and dreams for family and future.

Home Ownership's Advantages for Clergy

Which weighs more? The emotional or economic value of home ownership? We know "this world is not our home, we're just a-passin' through," that our life at no time consists of what we own. Looking at economic and even self-esteem issues of home ownership versus parsonage living seems superficial and unspiritual. Yet we are called to be good stewards of our lives and our resources, both as a church and as individuals.

Home ownership carries an emotional bonus for both pastor and family beyond the ability to choose the neighborhood, school district and home best suited to their needs. They feel able to settle into a community, work through church problems, connect with people, get involved. The probability of a longer stay may increase as well, which assures deeper ministry and effectiveness for the church and the community.

Many ministers feel incalculable relief at physically and visually separating from the church. Living off location makes it easier to relax, play ball in the yard, cut the grass, look scrubby on days off.

FOR THE PASTOR
1. What is the emotional value to you of home ownership?
2. How does your current church provide equity?

Family life may receive more attention when ministers live in their own homes rather than next door to church, with work visually intruding whenever they glance outside. Suddenly, they have freedom for a normal yard and home life. No interested parishioners look out the church window to check how long the pastor takes a break or who slammed a door or how often someone makes coffee. No one cluck-clucks at the teenager's too-loud music. People in parsonages may miss this normalcy to life. When the pastor purchases a home, assumptions change. The pastor's right to a private life becomes more accepted by the congregation.

Living in a place separate from church property gives pastors a chance to get to know people not associated with the church. This provides opportunities to witness because they are not known automatically as "the people from the parsonage." They are just "Zach and Donna" on an evening walk—impacting a neighborhood for Christ.

Economically, the most significant benefits for home-owning ministers are equity and tax-reduction. One minister purchased a modest home twenty-five years ago in a small suburb; the area became the fastest growing in the metropolitan area. Now paid off, the value rocketed from twenty-five thousand to four hundred thousand dollars. When the clergy couple leaves ministry they have a place to live or a nice nest egg for retirement should they move or downsize. They have collateral and a credit history, which many ministers do not.

In addition to building equity, Provident Mutual called purchasing a home "the most significant tax benefit for ministers." The IRS allows ministers to exclude from gross income for income tax purposes the lesser of

☐ the fair rental value of the house and furnishings plus cost of utilities;

☐ the amount of the designated housing allowance;

☐ the amount actually spent to provide a home.

The church must establish the amount in advance.

Home Ownership's Advantages for the Church

Home ownership guarantees a living arrangement appropriate for the pastor's needs. The church is not saddled with repairs of the home—no small monetary amount, since most parsonages are not new. And because the minister holds the mortgage, selling when the pastor moves is not the church's problem—although out of grace people in the congregation could help with referrals and so forth.

Relief comes from knowing that your pastor is set up for the future—a house is as valuable as a retirement fund or pension. Congregations know when they are not being faithful to the needs of their pastor, and adequately providing for the family grants clean hearts and pure service for all.

A housing system that allows the pastor to buy is good stewardship of the pastor by the church and returns the investment the pastor makes in the church.

Home Ownership's Disadvantages

For the pastor, saving a down payment takes time. With a pastor's average salary noticeably lower than that of people with similar education, putting together enough money to establish a decent mortgage payment and rate may be nearly impossible.

The mortgage may be larger than the church's housing allowance. The fair rental value of a parsonage may be less than a mortgage payment for a similar-sized home. The housing allowance should be—but may not be—adequate for both mortgage and utilities. If the minister stays the average of two or three years, very little principal gets paid before moving. Selling the home is also costly given the financial fees involved in listing with a realtor and closing costs.

With a long-term mortgage the majority of money goes toward interest, so equity accrues slowly. One member turned this problem into a promise, telling his pastor, "Find out how much it would cost to have a ten-year mortgage instead of a thirty-year."

The pastor, Blake, delayed investigating, knowing he couldn't afford the payment. The parishioner asked again. This time, Blake called the bank. When he reported back, his friend said, "I'll pay the monthly difference. Take out the ten-year loan so you'll build some equity." Blake and his wife were floored by the gift. In their seven years in that home, they saved tremendously on interest and built up significant equity.

FOR THE PASTOR

Whether parsonage or home ownership, what are your best memories within those walls?

What if the home doesn't sell when the pastor leaves? Bridge loans, renting out the home while awaiting a sale and renting a temporary place in the new area—these cost time and money. A Houston congregation solves the resale problem, buying the house from the pastor and then selling it themselves.

For the congregation, the largest disadvantages are monetary—they may not have budgeted for a housing allowance, especially if the church already owns a home for the pastor.

Utilities should be included in the compensation package, but that is also expensive.

If clergy home ownership seems to be where God is leading you in terms of providing well for your pastor, here are ways to work around the expense for all parties:

☐ Invite realtors in the congregation to pray about donating time and commission to the Lord via helping clergy find a home.

☐ Ask parishioners if they might help the pastor start a down payment fund. Loan it at a low- to no-interest rate, or donate it.

☐ Lawyers might donate time and legal fees involved in buying a home.

☐ Give beyond your tithe to help with the principal payment for a shorter-term mortgage.

Whether the pastor lives in a rental home, a parsonage or is a homeowner, there are many ways to show honor and support. Probably the best advice was given two thousand years ago: "You shall love the Lord your God with all your heart, soul, mind and strength." And "love your neighbor as yourself" (see Lk 10:27).

Keeping the Pastor We Love

How can I help make the pastor's home a place of comfort and welcome?

What skills might I offer—window treatments, construction stuff, interior design, space-saving ideas . . . ?

Do I even know the pastor's dreams for the home?

If we have a parsonage system, what provisions has our church made for the pastor's retirement and equity?

Does the church cover the added cost of social security tax (most employers cover part of this) on the minister's home, or does it come from the pastor's pocket?

Here is how I will pray for my pastor's home:

11

When the Ends Don't Meet

*Just as you excel in everything—in faith, in speech, in knowledge,
in complete earnestness and in your love for us—
see that you also excel in this grace of giving.*

2 CORINTHIANS 8:7

Thank you, sir. I appreciate your offer. No, we won't be
needing assistance at this time. Thank you though." Maria
spoke around the nausea rising in her throat, then hung up the
phone with a shaking hand. The local service group's annual
Thanksgiving call always disturbed and humiliated her. With
four children and a clergy salary that put them in line for free
lunches and public aid, their phone number was given out for
charity baskets at holiday time. Just like baskets her church
distributed, though no one there knew of the clergy family's situation. Shame burned her face. How could a minister work so
many hours, sacrifice so much and still qualify for food drives?

Unfortunately, Maria's situation is not an isolated example.
When speaking with Cindy and Dan, who pastor a church in

Michigan, I asked if they ever felt financially deprived. "Yes," Cindy answered. "When we get free lunches at school and when other churches buy us Christmas presents."

Ordained to Poverty?
Low pay is enough to keep some people out of ministry or to force them to revamp dreams in order to survive. Carol said, "I never wanted to marry a pastor because of my mother's PK stories. At first I avoided romantic involvement with Brian because he wanted to be a minister! When we started getting serious, I changed my major from vocal performance to education. That would give us stability and a profession to fall back on." They have gone on to do great work in their community; the church is growing, but even after fifteen years in ministry, they still struggle to make ends meet.

Other clergy, exhausted by the continual financial struggle, leave the ministry altogether. A pastor's vow to ordained ministry sometimes becomes the family's involuntary vow to poverty.

Jesus said in Matthew 6:21, "Where your treasure is, there your heart will be also." Our heart follows our treasures. If this is true, then the work of the kingdom of God is frequently not the congregation's treasure.

From Salvage Shops to Self-Esteem
The U.S. Department of Labor last decade ranked ministry among the top ten professions for earning potential based on education, yet ranks it with unskilled labor based on salary.[1] Barna Research discovered that while the year 2001 marked a record level in clergy compensation, senior pastors still earned nearly one-third less annually than other professionals with graduate-level degrees: $42,083 versus $60,000. Further, congregations expected their pastors to earn less, regardless of

family needs and student loans, because their pastors were in ministry.[2] Twenty percent of pastors surveyed said their low salary had a negative effect on their self-worth,[3] scraping away at the pastor and family. It makes sense, then, that 30 percent of all pastors who resign do so due to salary issues.[4]

"I'm embarrassed to be so obviously on the other end of the financial stick," wrote a woman in ministry, "especially since in all other ways we're peers with the people at church—socially, educationally, background-wise. We can't afford to socialize at our parishioners' levels." It's hard not to equate less pay with less value for even the most giving pastors. Salary issues become a war on self-esteem.

Other casualties occur as well. Many clergy spouses must work to cover ministry expenses and shortfalls. Others work to escape the pressure of the pastorate.

"Our salary is just not adequate," said Cindy, the clergy spouse from Michigan. "We have always needed a second job to make ends meet. I feel sad and resentful toward the church because of low pay and no pay, making two jobs necessary. Sometimes Dan works both jobs, sometimes both of us. Either way, it's had enormous ramifications on our self-esteem, our parenting, our marriage and the quality of our contribution to the church."

This seems logical. The more fragmented we are, the less time we have, the less attention we can give to anyone (including God), the more scattered and shallow our relationships, and

---

FACTS ON FILE

Seventy percent of pastors in one survey indicated that their financial package contributed to difficulty in their marriage.[5]

---

the more compromised, less imaginative, less energetic our gifts of time and talent to the church.

A poor compensation package hurts everyone. Deitra feels called to minister alongside her husband, is committed to being present to her children and their friends, and has chosen not to take a paying job on the side. But this has cost them. "We are living off the inheritance from my mother's estate." Pastors do not expect to get rich when entering ministry; however, they should not be living off an inheritance.

FOR THE PASTOR
1. How does your current salary and compensation feel to you?
2. What effect does the package have on your self-esteem, your spouse, your family, your ability to minister?
3. To whom do you talk about this?

Certainly underpaying the pastor is contrary to Scripture. First Timothy 5:17-18 states, "The elders who direct the affairs of the church well are worthy of double honor, especially those whose work is preaching and teaching. For the Scripture says, 'Do not muzzle the ox while it is treading out the grain,' and 'The worker deserves his wages.'"

Further, in the Old Testament provisions were to be made as follows:

> The priests, who are Levites . . . shall live on the offerings made to the LORD by fire, for that is their inheritance. . . . This is the share due the priests: . . . you are to give them the firstfruits of your grain, new wine and oil, and the first wool from the shearing of your sheep, for the LORD your God has chosen them and their descendants out of all your tribes to stand and minister in the LORD's name always. (Deut 18:1, 3-5)

While as followers of Christ we are not bound by Old Testament law, the honor that was accorded priests then carries through to today. This is clear in the Timothy passage. Unfortunately, the concept of firstfruits, or of tithing ten percent, has been lost in many churches, and "the offerings made to the Lord" by the people are often not enough to meet a bare-bones church budget, let alone sustain a minister and family.

The result nowadays is remarkably similar to what happened in the Old Testament. When the people failed to support the priests and Levites, the ordained left their ministries and went to work in the fields. Nehemiah 13:10 says, "The portions assigned to the Levites had not been given to them, and . . . all the Levites and singers responsible for the service had gone back to their own fields." Ministers today may carry two jobs, spouses are working, and families are being shredded by the time spent scratching out a living. Pastors leave the ministry, exhausted by the constant financial stress.

So why don't we just give 'em a raise?

Now, About That Raise, Pastor

Finances seem to be a nationwide concern for clergy families. Half the clergy wives surveyed by the Alban Institute had major concerns about finances.[6] In the last decade, four-tenths of pastors felt underpaid; their median income was fourteen thousand dollars less than their lay colleagues in church leadership.[8]

"We were hurt when two different professionals at church asked us to pray that they would get a raise," Barry and Nora said. "We knew they voted to 'hold the line' on our salary when we asked for a salary increase." They pastor in a large denomination, yet have struggled financially in every church, with a salary always far below the denominational minimum. The church's failure to provide adequately for their pastor remains a mystery.

"In our second church," wrote Kim, "we used up all our savings just to get by. The senior pastor, learning this, recommended a large raise. The congregation came through." Thanks be to God that the church realized that "a worker is worthy" of wages. Failure to provide materially for the needs of God's anointed and appointed contradicts scriptural admonitions to care for those in ministry.

Barriers to Raises

There are numerous barriers to raises. Misinformation is one: many ministers do not receive raises because the parishioners do not really understand their needs. Making those needs known is a first step. Likewise, hesitation on the part of clergy may keep them from getting an increase.[9] Many leave a church instead of asking for a raise. One survey found that 10 percent of pastors would have their spouses find a job rather than seek a deserved raise.[10]

Perhaps the church does not have a policy in place for raises. In one church where my husband served, no one had received a raise in fifteen years. Frozen salaries are not uncommon, even in upper-income areas with large churches and multiple staff. While some denominations have base-level standards for their pastors, others do not; frequently, independent churches do not include this in their by-laws. A three-percent cost of living raise should be required.

Sometimes a barrier may be control or just plain nosiness by the church board. One minister said, "Our board was happy to talk about a raise. But first, I had to show them every check, every bill, every statement, every need. I had to justify every cent I spent." Some information is helpful, but no one has the right to demand this kind of proof of financial need. Such indignity would never happen in another job setting.

Perhaps shame about debt creates reluctance in clergy about asking for a raise. Said Margaret, "We've lived our lives with short-term goals and long-term debt. Now, a decade away from retirement, we are finally beginning to consider how and where we will live."

FOR THE PASTOR
1. Be honest with church leaders—if you are mired in debt and it's an emotional load, be up front with them.
2. Ask for financial accountability, and for help.
3. If your compensation is unrealistic, come to the board with a plan for bringing it gradually (or immediately!) up to realistic standards.

But Is It Spiritual?

Money is a hot issue in marriages and in churches. Many pastors will not ask for a raise because they do not want to risk their spiritual connection with the church board. (See how frequently Jesus talked about money in the Gospels. It was one hot topic for him as well—but he dared to mention it!)

Boards may recite the mantra "We just can't afford a raise." We are back to the concept of tithing again. It is speculated that churches that tithe should never have a problem with adequate compensation.

Remember God's promise to the Israelites? "'Bring the whole tithe into the storehouse, so that there may be food in My house, and test Me now in this,' says the LORD of hosts, 'if I will not open for you the windows of heaven, and pour out for you a blessing until there is no more need" (Mal 3:10 NASB).

In 2 Chronicles 31, Hezekiah was at the head of a great revival in Israel. They re-instituted the offerings and the tithe, and the people "brought a great amount, a tithe of everything . . . and they piled them in heaps" (vv. 5-6). So much came in that they had to prepare storerooms! Azariah the chief priest said, "Since the people began to bring their contributions to the temple of the LORD, we have had enough to eat and plenty to spare, because the LORD has blessed his people, and this great amount is left over" (v. 10).

Changing the Bottom Line Without Breaking the Budget (Or Even Increasing It)

How do we "test God now in this"? Any church, even the financially strapped, can boost the pastor's bottom line, and thus the self-esteem quotient, and lower the stress level without holding bake sales or starting a pledge campaign for the salary. Knowing we are meeting specific clergy needs feels good; we are blessed in the giving, and relationships between congregation and pastor are enhanced. These suggestions may also reduce the amount of taxes clergy shell out, thus increasing take-home pay.[11]

Salary reduction by tithe. This seems backward, doesn't it? Because they do not have enough deductions to qualify, many clergy do not file the long form for taxes and cannot then deduct their giving from taxable salary. Pastors who tithe to the church can elect to lower their salary by ten percent at the beginning, and then there is no tax to be paid because they never received that ten percent in the first place. This transaction should be in writing and in church minutes to maintain a record of the original salary.

Cafeteria plan. Under section 125 in the IRS code, the employer offers all paid ministers the possibility of setting aside money from the cash salary and putting it into an account for medical expenses, including health insurance, dental and eyecare. The total amount set aside is excluded from the pastor's 1099 form. However, any monies not used are lost under the "use it or lose it" rule.

Note: This does not cost the church any extra money; it simply allows ministers to exclude medical expenses from their gross income before filing with the IRS. Also, the cafeteria plan must be administered through the proper channels, using a section 125 plan administrator. Check with your financial adviser for details.

Time-share. When Kay and Max badly needed a vacation, a church member offered them free use of their time-share vacation spot. Often people who buy these packages don't use them; how about donating a visit to your pastor? That way a vacation is provided, but it doesn't cost the church an additional raise. Or give the pastor an extra week off each year with pay. It costs the church nothing but feels like a raise to clergy.

Pastor's aid fund. Parishioners are invited to contribute to a fund which goes toward special needs of the staff.

Parishioner support. In one Chicago-area congregation, less than one hundred members support a growing staff. The compensation package comprises money from the budget and specific line items pledged by parishioners: the cell phone base price, the home phone local call package, Internet connection, even automobile reimbursement. These are provided to the pastor as specific gifts from people in the church. If books are your passion, perhaps you would want to set up a book fund for the staff. The ways of giving are limitless, the joy provided both giver and receiver boundless.

Here's another possibility for giving. "[Peter] stayed many days in Joppa with a certain tanner, Simon, . . . whose house is by the sea" (Acts 9:43; 10:6 NASB). One family gave a modern Peter and his family exclusive use of their swimming pool one day a week. Linda and Cal were given two weeks at a family's lake cottage every year. Sounds like a house by the sea to me! (For other ideas, visit the IVP website at <www.ivpress.com>.)

However you choose to love God by sharing with the minister, be creative. Have fun. Let the joy of the Lord flow through you as you give honor to your pastor. And may it be returned to you a hundredfold. May the windows of heaven open upon you and rain down blessing.

Keeping the Pastor We Love

When have I reviewed the salary and compensation information provided for my pastor? How does that rank with the average income in our congregation? In our community?

What is my church's policy on raises? Is there a denominational minimum? How do we care for our clergy comparatively?

Where am I in my giving? What percent is it of my income?

What is God leading me to do in the area of finances for the minister? Are there gifts or services I can share to help even out the budget?

Here's how I will pray for my clergy about their income needs:

12

Building Better Clergy Compensation

Give, and it will be given to you; good measure, pressed down, shaken together,
running over, they will pour into your lap. For whatever measure you deal out
to others, it will be dealt to you in return.

LUKE 6:38 (NASB)

We met Quinn when talking about the twin destroyers of stress and burnout. At the highest-stress point of ministry, this pastor from the South found no one to talk with, no one to share the fear, anger and lack of expertise he felt. Within weeks, Quinn became another statistic when he died of a massive coronary. Dead at age fifty, his body is buried in a rural cemetery. His wife and seven children, who had been squeezed into a three-bedroom parsonage, were literally homeless because no equity had been set aside by the church to purchase a home.

When the church members were asked to contribute financially to the pastor's family in a time of near destitution and desperate grief, they answered, "She'll get social security."

This seems irrational and stone-cold (it is both), and it is far from bestowing honor on our pastor; yet few topics are more inflammatory than money. And few places are more incendiary than the church and the pastor's compensation package. How can we bless our clergy financially?

"But the Pastor's Making Lots of Money!"

"Why should we give the pastor a raise?" asked a professor who sat on the finance board. "Why, our minister makes the same as I do."

Several others nodded. Buzzing sounded. People compared bottom lines. The problem: no one defined bottom line, and the bottom line for pastors is different from that of other employees because their compensation package is arranged differently.

"Compensation package" typically includes salary plus non-cash benefits. Many boards compare a pastor's salary with their own take-home pay and believe that the pay is similar; however, most employers cover expenses for their employees *prior* to payday—expenses that pastors frequently pay for themselves *after* cashing their paycheck. For instance, health insurance, business expenses, entertainment and travel typically come out of the pastor's take-home pay rather than the employer's coffers. Also, for social security purposes ministers are considered self-employed and thus must pay their own social security taxes; usually an employer pays for half of this.

So out of that paycheck, which at first glance seemed comparable to church members', the pastor pays 15.3 percent of cash salary plus housing allowance for social security, approximately 15 percent for federal taxes and 9 percent for state taxes, unreimbursed travel, business/professional expenses, ministry-related hospitality/entertainment, and the cost of health insurance . . . and then is expected to live on the rest. (See appendix D for a budgeting chart.)

The Compensation Package

The discrepancy is easily remedied, but it may take time to bring the pastor's package up to par for your community and the pastor's experience. The clergy compensation package includes several standard items

Medical expenses/insurance. When we first entered the ministry fifteen years ago, medical insurance was around a hundred dollars a month. Now it can cost a thousand or more per month depending on the plan type, group size, deductible and specific benefits. This gobbles up an enormous amount of a minister's salary. Churches should do all they can to be certain their pastoral family has adequate coverage for health and dental insurance and eye care, including it in the budget. Or consider a higher deductible with resultant lower premiums and then pay for the deductible as a church. Or several churches could band together and create a "group," thus qualifying for better rates. However you make it work, do it out of faithfulness to God. The cost of going without insurance is far too high, and too many clergy do just that. (See the discussion of cafeteria plans in chapter eleven, "When the Ends Don't Meet," for ideas on how to maximize the minister's take-home pay.)

Life insurance. Often a line item in the budget, life insurance can be part of compensation. The cost of term life can be excluded from the minister's salary, covered by the church budget or even picked up by a parishioner. The average pastor is a forty-four-year-old, nonsmoking male; $100,000 term life coverage for a twenty-year policy is $430 a year or $39.00 a month. For ten years, the rate locks in at $26 a month.[1]

IRS regulations. Under current IRS regulations, an employer may provide as a benefit up to $50,000 of term insurance at no tax cost to the employee. The church, at a small cost, could provide this insurance with no income tax or social security cost to the pastor. If church funds are tight, the church and the minister can agree to reduce the salary by the cost of such term insurance and then provide it as a benefit at no cost to the church, while still being tax-free to the pastor.

Worker compensation insurance. In most states, such coverage is required, particularly if the church has other employees; this protects pastors and their families in the event of a costly accident, disability or death. "Some states may not require a church to take out such insurance if the pastor is the only employee, yet the church (the employer/salary-paying unit) is still held liable for all such costs due to accident while the pastor (employee) is going about the business of the employer (the church)," says Rev. Charles Chakour, former treasurer of the Northern Illinois Conference of the United Methodist Church and author of the book *Building Clergy Compensation.* "It is wise for churches to protect themselves and their pastor from such damages and costs when the annual cost of protection is so small (in most instances, only a few cents per hundred dollars of total compensation, which should always include salary, benefits and housing at the least)."

Travel allowance. Pastors drive thousands of miles for the church each year, often without reimbursement. They shuttle members on mission and youth trips, sometimes many hours away, without compensation. The wear and tear on the car is costly and quickly diminishes its life. Twenty years ago it cost an estimated $.50 per mile to drive a car. This included repairs, maintenance, gas and so on. Adding in inflation, the actual driving cost far exceeds the amount allowed by the IRS for deduction, currently at 36.5 cents per mile.

Churches can reimburse the pastor for mileage, parking and tolls through an expense account. With highly fluctuating gas

costs, figure on 36.5 cents per mile and 12,500 miles per year
for starters. A congregational member might want to cover this
expense on a year-by-year basis.

Car allowance. Some churches provide both a car and reimbursement for mileage. Others set up a car fund, allowing the
pastor to purchase the car from that fund. Melinda was given a
new car of her choosing by her church in Wisconsin. If the
church budget can't sustain the cost of a car, consider this possibility: in one of our churches, a generous family who owned a
car dealership provided a business car for each minister as part
of their tithe. God's grace through this family left us speechless
with gratitude.

Housing allowance. A typical housing allowance should be
the median worth of the homes in the community and the
church members' homes, plus utilities. Some churches that do
not offer a housing allowance but instead install their minister
in a parsonage will put into a separate "equity" account for the
pastor a set sum of money each month for the eventual purchase of a home. This is tax free when withdrawn if used for
the purchase of a house. The Episcopal Church recommends
setting aside 5 to 10 percent of total compensation as tax-
deferred if the cleric lives in church-owned housing.[2] (See
chapter ten, "Hearth and Home.")

Continuing education. Certainly churches will want to provide for the continued enrichment, learning and spiritual nourishment of their clergy. The typical yearly allocation for
continuing education is not enough to cover even one graduate
level course. One church-required conference can chew up
most continuing education allowances without being a true
continuing ed expense.

To rectify this a church can establish a continuing ed fund
(one suggestion: set the amount at the cost of a graduate level

course) and a separate fund for church-mandated conferences. A Messianic church in the Midwest makes funds available for additional course or degree work after two years of employment with the congregation; seminar and conference stipends are separate items in the budget.

An Ohio parishioner gave a year's tuition for a special clergy growth program; the following year, he split the cost for that with the church and a continuing education fund. Watching his pastor apply new truth to ministry gives this member much happiness; he frequently comments with enthusiasm, "I can see where this is helping your work."

Hospitality/Entertainment. Clergy are expected to minister through hospitality; a line item compensating them for the use of home and gifts is reasonable. This allows pastors the freedom to "treat" others without penalizing their own needs and the family budget.

Salary exclusions. If the minister determines in advance how much will be spent on pension, life insurance, and business and professional expenses, these can be excluded from the gross income reported to the IRS. This action must be voted on by the board and be recorded in board minutes. These monies also fall under the "use it or lose it" rule: any dollar amount declared but not spent will not be returned to the pastor.

FACTS ON FILE

Sixty-three percent of pastors in Leadership's *1997 survey indicated that they practice a pre-tax, 10-percent tithe; 76 percent practice either a pre- or post-tax tithe of 10 percent.[3] Many pastors I interviewed tithe 20 to 30 percent of their income.*

A Word on Retirement

"Why should we give our minister a housing allowance?" the chair of the staff-church relations board from a local church asked at a training event.

"Because if you don't provide ministers with equity now, they will have no place to live when they retire. Or they will be slammed with a $200,000 mortgage to carry until they die," I answered.

"They call retired ministers 'the new homeless,'" a pastor from South Dakota said.

The chair of that board went back to the church, and the church voted to provide a housing allowance in lieu of a parsonage for the pastor. That was a vote of faithfulness to the minister for the long haul.

A pastor from Louisiana wrote, "I have always been apprehensive and hesitant to put a price upon my ministry, thus, I was very negligent in securing adequate finances in the first 20 years of pastoring. (Nevertheless, the Lord always met our needs and more.) In my third church, the Board of Deacons finally inquired regarding my retirement program which at that point was zero. I had none. They were very surprised. For the last six years of a 16-year ministry they offered to match a percentage of our monthly salaries set aside for retirement, up to 7%. I chose the maximum. They made the same offer to all six staff members."

FOR THE PASTOR
1. What plans have you made for retirement beyond social security?
2. Where will you live? At what monthly income after retirement?
3. Would it be wise to meet with a financial planner and consider additional plans to provide more adequately for those years?

Many denominations have pension programs and annuities, some of which are paid mutually between church and pastor. I applaud them for thinking of the long-term welfare of their pastors by providing for retirement. The matching funds program (above) is a good start in honoring the pastor's current investment in ministry with future provisions.

If the denomination does not have an official pension program (and I would have to ask "Why not?" of the people in the hierarchy overseeing the pastor's care), begin one for your local church. Likely someone in your church has connections with financial advisers or investors and can direct your pastor and board to wisely invest these funds so they will grow steadily until retirement.

IRS regulations let ministers exclude up to $10,500 of annual income for investment in tax-sheltered (403B) annuities (tax free) beyond the employer's pension plan. Any dollar amount above that is taxable. Provided they have stayed in the same denomination, people who are employed by churches, conventions and church-controlled groups can also opt for the "catch-up elective" for years when salary was low and little put into pension. This allows pastors to set aside larger amounts of income without tax.[4] Further, clergy over age fifty can set aside an additional amount beyond the $10,500 limit. Check with your tax adviser for the specifics of these options.

When pastors give the best years of life to the church, we want to give them more than a going-away party at retirement. Or a tombstone.

Vows and Responsibility: A Three-Way Deal

"All this talk of money and the ministry." "Filthy lucre!" "You cannot serve both God and Mammon!" "Money is the root of all evil." (Actually, the Scripture reads, "The love of money . . . ") Why spend all this energy talking about money? Partly because the days are gone when pastors can pay their doctor bill with a double-yolk egg. But don't we believe in Jehovah Jireh? Yes, God will provide. And when ministers vow to serve God through serving the church, they trust that God will provide for them through the very institutions they serve.

> I am to be the only inheritance the priests have. . . . I will be their possession. They will eat the grain offerings, the sin offerings and the guilt offerings; and everything in Israel devoted to the LORD will belong to them. The best of all the firstfruits and of all your special gifts will belong to the priests. You are to give them the first portion of your ground meal so that a blessing may rest on your household. (Ezek 44:28-30)

It's really a three-party contract: the Levites declare God their only inheritance and give themselves totally to the Lord's service; God guarantees to be their possession; and the people of the church promise to provide for the priests from the firstfruits, the very best, of all their stuff so that the givers and their households will in turn be blessed. The blessing of giving continues in the New Testament as well:

> Remember this: Whoever sows sparingly will also reap sparingly, and whoever sows generously will also reap generously. Each . . . should give what he has decided in his heart to give, not reluctantly or under compulsion, for God loves a cheerful giver. And God is able to make all grace abound to you, so that in all things at all times, having all that you need, you will abound in every good work. (2 Cor 9:6-8)

Giving results in grace, provision and further ministry! What a bargain!

Serving the Servant

When the dentist said our three children needed braces, my stomach rolled. We were at such a low point financially that I reacted physiologically to the news. We visited a recommended orthodontist—and left, reeling from his fees. I wondered how to pay for one child's braces, let alone three.

FOR THE PASTOR
1. When has God provided for your needs anonymously? Or by people outside the church?
2. How has people's giving to you increased your joy for ministry? Your family's love for God? When was the last time you told your congregation that?
3. Pray for the people who have given to you of their gifts—time, talents, treasures.

A year later, the dentist warned, new referrals in hand, "They really must get started." I sought the proper orthodontist critically and methodically: which one was closer for us? Still, walking into the office for the first visit with two children in tow, I felt an unusual flood of assurance, the kind that comes from God. This was right: Game Boys for patients, coffee machine (free!) for parents, even a free concert-ticket raffle for a wildly popular band—this orthodontist cared about patients.

Our meeting and initial examinations confirmed this. His manner with my kids was a parent's dream. We found extracurricular Christian activities and connections in common. This doctor was a believer! More assurance, so strongly I blinked back tears.

Then the doctor said, "Your dental insurance requires that you see a network provider—and I am unfortunately out of the network. But we can work out payments." I felt sick to have missed this detail. "I'm so sorry. Please forgive me for taking up your time. I can't believe I forgot to check into providers." Without any insurance help, it was impossible financially. I began gathering belongings.

His lively office manager directed his attention to the intake sheet. The doctor glanced down, then asked, "What does your husband do?"

"He's a pastor."

"Oh! Forget everything I said about money. I never charge clergy."

Even my kids were stunned silent. Then I did cry, still trying to speak coherently. "How can you do that? You care so much for pastors and their families that you would cover their orthodontia? You don't even know us! And we have three children!"

Later he said, "I call it 'Serve the Servant'. I just want to return to ministers a portion of what they give."

Another day, in the waiting room I looked up to find the doctor at my shoulder, grinning. "Pastor So and So just stopped in for a consultation. We were their third stop." And their last, I might add, judging by the joy on the doctor's face at being able to care, once again, for the caregiver.

Whatever your area of expertise or passion, might God be calling you to make a gift of that gift to your minister? Honoring the clergy family will result in blessing beyond belief—for the pastor, the family, the church and for you.

Provide well for your pastors, that the blessing of the Lord might "rest on your household."

Keeping the Pastor We Love

Which parts of the compensation package possibilities are currently in place for my pastor? How adequate are they?

How are we providing for our clergy's retirement? Can we set up a matching-equity plan?

What is the housing setup, and what are my pastor's plans for retirement?

When have I experienced the blessing of God resting on my

household because of my giving?

When have I tested out the truth of Luke 6:38, "Give, and it will be given to you"? How is my standard of measure?

Here's how I will pray for my pastor regarding finances:

13

Crisis Care

*Praise be to the God and Father of our Lord Jesus Christ,
the Father of compassion and the God of all comfort,
who comforts us in all our troubles, so that we can comfort those
in any trouble with the comfort we ourselves have received from God.*

2 CORINTHIANS 1:3-4

When the pain stabbed my chest, I breathed through it like any three-time Lamaze veteran. The pain continued, increasing with each breath. My three small children and my parents surrounded the table at the café in colonial Williamsburg. Only Rich was missing from the gathering; with no more vacation days for the year, he had been tuning in long distance to our travelogue for a week.

Inside the dim café, my food cooled in its pewter dish. My mother noticed my unusual lack of appetite. "Honey, you are as white as a sheet. Are you okay?"

Of course I was. I was always okay. Besides, we were on vacation.

Minutes later, I was stretched out on an old, quaint plank in the lobby, ambulance technicians hovering overhead. My children crowded around my folks at the doorway. Anxiety covered all five faces.

The stabbing pain eluded lobby diagnosis. "Did you strain a muscle during exercise, ma'am?" the attendant asked. I nearly laughed, but it hurt too much. Instead, I gasped, "I don't think so."

"Lady, we're taking you in." It was not a question.

"In where?" I couldn't quite get the plan.

"To the hospital."

"You can't take me to the hospital. Just fix me here."

"Lady, do you know what's wrong with you?"

That silenced my ever-moving mouth. "No," I said, now meek.

"Neither do we. We're taking you in."

First trip to Williamsburg, first ride in an ambulance, first non-childbirth hospitalization . . . it was only the beginning of vacation firsts. Twenty-four hours after a grueling battery of tests, they had the diagnosis: pulmonary embolism in my right lung. Prescription: a week in the hospital, blood thinners administered intravenously, oxygen until the pain dissipated, no vitamin K-laden (blood-thickening) foods.

With Rich hundreds of miles away, my children and parents stuck (though not complaining) in a tourist city on the Fourth of July in triple-digit heat, I felt helpless and hopeless for the first time. The bedside phone rang. My husband's voice came through: "Should I fly down? Someone from the church offered plane fare." The generosity further took my breath away. We debated, then decided care surrounded me in the hospital. I would need help more back home.

The auxiliary lady in crisp pink and white breezed into the room on the third day. "Mail call," she chirped. I looked at her, concerned for her sanity. Clearly she had the wrong room. "Aren't you Jane Rubietta?" I checked my wristband. Nodded.

"Well, these are for you." She handed me a passel of mail, all from parishioners in Joliet, Illinois—concerned, loving me cross-country.

Hospitals tend to move patients toward weeping and depression. Weeping started when people began caring. My prayer partner called, "What can I do?" My writer buddies phoned, "Let us help when you get back." The women's group organized meals following my return. Others volunteered daily childcare for several hours. My sister and her husband took off work and drove all day to rescue my children. A former pastor called, praying with me on the phone.

This time, when the pastor's family was in crisis the church responded with love and action. I will never forget the feeling of being cared for in tangible ways. Months later, a dear woman said after church one Sunday, "I still pray for you every day. Do you remember to take your blood-thinners?"

"I do, Katherine, and I think of you. Please don't stop praying for me," I think even now.

Name-a-Crisis

Whatever the problem, the minister and family are not exempt. Pastors encounter exactly the same crises as parishioners, whether concerning health, marriage, children, in-laws, finances or spiritual/emotional burnout. Addiction, compulsive behavior, depression . . . the list is as long as the church roll. A minister's position does not guarantee a pain-free existence.

FACTS ON FILE

Seventy-five percent of clergy report regular periods of major distress.[1]

When Fred received word that his mother had been killed in a car wreck, he and Hazel sat alone in their dark house, curtains closed. Numb with grief, their position as pastoral couple totally isolated them. No one in the church dared to help the professionals at caring.

When Bill and Susan miscarried their baby, the church board expected Bill in the pulpit the next Sunday, as usual. He broke down mid-sermon. "The church did not understand our grief. Most minimized and misunderstood our loss. Few people had real compassion for us. I chose to worship somewhere else," said Susan, sadness still wreathing her face.

FOR THE PASTOR
1. When has the church failed to care for you in crisis?
2. How did you communicate your problems and needs to them?
3. How and when has the body of Christ come through in difficult times?
4. How do you feel about receiving help?

When LaTanya was hospitalized for a month for depression, family therapy was necessary, and the facility was ninety minutes away. Her mother, Angela, pastor of a large church in Maryland, told a select few on the church board that she needed time for family healing. The board rallied, interpreted the problem carefully to members, took over pastoral care functions and granted Angela all the time necessary to recover.

911—Help

How can—how should—how must the church respond to a crisis in the pastor's life or family? The "one another" passages again point us in the right direction (see appendix B, "Bible Study on Loving Your Pastor"). How has our minister cared for us in a tough time? Weep with those who weep. Strengthen the ankles that are weak. Comfort one another with the same comfort we have received.

I feel inept and deficient at helping people who are wiser and deeper than I am. What do you say to the person who uses words and the Word professionally? What can lay people say to the ordained caregiver? How about . . . nothing? Sometimes the greatest gift is wordless. Henri Nouwen says:

> The friend who can be silent with us in a moment of despair or confusion, who can stay with us in an hour of grief and bereavement, who can tolerate not knowing, not-curing, not-healing and face with us the reality of our powerlessness, that is the friend who cares. . . . The friend who makes it clear that whatever happens in the external world, being present to each other is what really matters.[2]

Beyond physical presence, how do we overwhelm a pastor with love in a crisis, or in the subsequent recovery period, when the rest of the world is back to normal but family fallout continues? A card, a phone call, a hot meal, a surprise gift, an offer to baby sit, a phone card, the gift of space and healing time, a certificate for a hotel getaway or massage, maid service, lawn care, rides to therapy or the doctor, groceries delivered to the door: there is no end to the ways we can minister grace and love to clergy and family in their hour of need.

Because compassion and creativity go hand in hand to help loved ones through a difficult season, we must ask: Do we really consider our pastor and family "loved ones"? Once Patti knew I was in a tough spot, and she delivered a cup of foaming cappuccino coffee. Another time in crisis, Rich and I came home late at night and found our table set for a romantic dinner, the crock pot simmering, candles waiting and a loving note from our friend in Christ who had been tending the house in our absence. We were considered "loved ones."

In addition to not knowing how to support clergy in crisis, we aren't always aware that our pastors have little support. No one is singing "Lean on Me" to most ministers. This may be the only difference between a clergy crisis and parishioner crisis: the clergy have no caregivers to uphold them. This void delays, if not totally hinders, the healing that is necessary. In *Stress in the Ministry,* Mills and Koval write, "Consistently, those who report self-support—that is, no sources of support beyond themselves—reported fewer successful outcomes in the succeeding period. It seems that stress is hardest to resolve when external support is absent."[3]

Along with practical support, another means of comforting is often overlooked. One possibility, a brief or even extended leave to recover, is rarely mentioned by minister or member.

> Churches would do well to consider formal leaves of absence . . . for pastors who experience a personal crisis. Too many times, a conscientious pastor will precipitously leave the ministry during a personal crisis rather than ask for a time away to work things out.[4]

Why wouldn't a minister feel free to ask for space for healing from a church? Have we created an accepting and grace-full place for our pastors, a place where another's problems are not interpreted as a sign of sin but as an opportunity to hold one another before God and administer aid? Even exemplary Job was not excluded from suffering. His friends failed the "comfort one another" test; hopefully we can improve on their record!

Kids in Crisis and Special-Needs Kids

"This has been the hardest year of my life," said Judy, a pastor's spouse in New York. "My mother died, we've had three weddings in our family, and my son and new daughter-in-law told us right after the ceremony that she was three months pregnant." Tears of pain and bewilderment surfaced. "We raised our children well; they know the Lord, know right from wrong and certainly knew about the sanctity of marriage. Still, we worried about repercussions. Though the newlyweds lived an hour away, what would the church do if they learned our son got a girl pregnant? We told the elders, then sent a letter to every church member telling them the situation."

In this instance, the pastor's ministry was not jeopardized because of a son's actions; Judy and Randy simply wanted to be up front about the crisis in their home. No one can help if no one knows the problems. And the church extended grace to this family, grace to the couple who conceived outside the bonds of marriage but then cemented their commitment with a wedding. The church's love to the entire family modeled Christ's love for the newlyweds, leading them back to church.

This is not always the way it works. Many pastors dread misbehavior or even a crisis of faith on the part of their children, fearing that their job is in danger. While we know the stipulation for the minister's family in Scripture (see 1 Tim 3:4-5), at some point children must be given credit—or made to bear the responsibility—for their own choices and free will. Rebellious children complicate and jeopardize their own futures; their parents' jobs should not be compromised because of children's poor choices. Would plumbers lose their jobs because their kids clogged someone's toilet or TP'd a football player's house? Probably not.

Some kid crises are short lived. Some are long term. One of Dave and Teresa's twins died at birth. The surviving child had multiple health challenges, and Teresa's ministry in the local church was abbreviated because of their child's needs. Likewise, Dave's job description needed adjustment so he could do physical therapy for the little boy as he grew, and relieve Teresa from the emotional and physical strain of constant care. All this on top of grieving the twin's death.

Understanding that they were partners for the long haul, the church supported them, rotated help and provided breaks for the clergy couple. Dave and Teresa continue to minister today because the church became extended family, adjusted expectations and committed themselves to "one another" care.

Do your pastors have special-needs children? Whether AD/HD, Down's Syndrome, hearing- or sight-impaired, learning or physical disability, asthma, how can the church help? One church quietly put an extra helper in each Sunday school classroom for a boy with severe hyperactivity.

Wise Emergency Planning

Life stress and trauma are inevitable; preparing wisely is the responsibility of both church and pastor. One practical option is including short-term disability insurance in the clergy compensation package. To allow for 70 percent of pay, up to $1,000 per week, should be around $360 per year, less than $10 per week, according to one financial planner who works with ministers. Making certain that our clergy have adequate health and life insurance is vital—especially since long-term health care problems can cripple a pastor's finances and ministry.

Another possibility: providing worker's comp for pastors, a fairly standard provision for many employees. This covers them for any accident occurring while on the job, including visitation travel. (See chapter twelve, "Building Better Clergy Compensation.")

Some denominations establish a fund for minister emergencies. The United Church of Christ has a donation category to help retired pastors and spouses. In one church, a wealthy member gave beyond his tithe to set up a "slush fund" which could be used for a variety of special needs and crises for staff members or parishioners.

Call Me Joy

The church, unfortunately, may add to the weight of ministry and even contribute to family pain. We also know that heavy expectations and long work hours pull pastors' families apart. Without an adequate financial package, spouses must work to supplement benefits and paycheck, further splintering the family. And with nowhere to turn for counseling, no safe place for help, the family plummets more deeply into despair.

"Weeping may last for the night, but a shout of joy comes in the morning" (Ps 30:5 NASB). As with laity, the pastor's night may be very long and very dark, and the weeping profuse. "I am worn out from groaning; all night long I flood my bed with weeping and drench my couch with tears," King David cried (Ps 6:6).

Are we up to the task? Can we hold on to our beloved leaders—or learn to love them through holding—throughout their own dark night of the soul? Can we be joy for them, holding them close to God through prayer, strengthening them through practical gifts of service, embracing them in wordless empathy and compassion for their pain?

The Scriptures promise that one day "God will wipe away every tear from their eyes" (Rev 7:17), and that "there will be no more death or mourning or crying or pain" (Rev 21:4). Until that glorious, clear-eyed day, however, we are called to bear one another's burdens—including those of our clergy and families. So let's grab a tissue, or lend a hammer and a hand, or write a note, or turn on the oven to make that specialty item . . . and watch joy come in the morning.

Keeping the Pastor We Love

When have I wondered if my pastor or family might be troubled or in a crisis, and not acted?

What are my most comfortable ways of helping? How could I do some "one another" caring for my minister?

Would I question my minister's ability to lead because of a clergy kid-crisis?

Do my pastor's children have special needs? How can I help?

How could I help in a long-term crisis to relieve stress and exhaustion? What signs should I be looking for in my pastor and family?

How have we as a church helped plan wisely in the event of an emergency for our minister? Do we have worker's comp, life and disability insurance, pension? With whom should I discuss this so we are good stewards of our pastor?

Here's how I will pray for my pastor:

14

Great Goodbyes

In your unfailing love you will lead
the people you have redeemed.
In your strength you will guide them
to your holy dwelling.

EXODUS 15:13

The offertory approached. The congregation looked eagerly at their gifted worship minister, Scott, anticipating his final trumpet solo. Instead, an unknown man stepped to the organ. Scott sat in the front row, knowing that the organist would replace him within a few weeks.

When the choir prepared to sing, Scott continued to sit in his pew. Again the stranger ascended the platform, this time conducting the choir anthem. The congregation rustled. What was happening?

The head pastor introduced, in glowing terms, their new worship leader; he did not mention the farewell reception following the service for Scott and his family.

At the reception, Scott and Nancy stood along one wall of the fellowship hall saying their goodbyes, even as the senior minister again introduced the replacement and gave him the stage.

That day, Nancy vowed, "I will never set foot in that church again." Now, several years later, she says, "Hurting me is one thing; hurting my husband, who worked at substandard pay for years, taking incessant side jobs, sacrificing family time to cover our most basic needs . . . there's no excuse for the rudeness and thoughtlessness." She has since forgiven and found closure, but the damage done in that one worship service lasted for years in both the church and the pastor's family.

With frequent clergy moves, closure is vital for ministers and their congregations. Those final weeks in a church provide beautiful opportunities for the church to overwhelm clergy with "love and appreciation."

Closing the Wound

Closure involves work and pain: thinking through grief issues, regrets, hopes. Avoiding closure, though, is like leaving a gash open and festering, then pretending it doesn't hurt or even exist. Healing, for church and pastor, takes a long time when denial is the chosen route. Wrote Mary, "I never said a real goodbye to the people I loved at that church. I still grieve over that. And I always felt like both a coward and a sneak, avoiding my loss and the discomfort I felt with my own weepiness and with theirs." Here's why we need closure.

☐ Closure signifies completion. "We have come full circle."

☐ Closure marks a place of significance, like the Israelites building altars and monuments in the wilderness. "God has done something here. We celebrate that."

☐ Closure demonstrates people's importance, their contributions to life, growth and the furthering of God's work and will in this world.

☐ Closure honors people's commitment and their feelings.

Creating opportunities for closure is a bit like cleaning up after ourselves or finishing a task to make the way ready for the one to follow. Lack of closure denies others' significance, which is dishonest and leads to a breech or break inside. Both Mary and her church could have avoided their guilt and loss; instead, they felt their own betrayal and lack of integrity—the sense of doing what is consistent with beliefs and needs—for years to come.

FOR THE PASTOR
1. When have you chosen to slip off, not emoting, trying to stay in control?
2. How did this help or hinder your grieving? Your family's grieving?
3. When have you carried bitterness and resentment off with you in a move?
4. How can you process those feelings in a healthy way?

Better to do the hard work up front, though hurtful, than to pack up our regrets and store them in the basement of our hearts or haul them with us. Unfortunately, one temptation for the congregation is to distance, to stop investing, to withdraw from relationships with the minister or family. Now is not the time for that! This is the time to uphold and care intensely.

"Be Attitudes" for Moving

For a church in transition, busyness is an easy escape hatch. A few "be attitudes" will help us stay on track with healthy grieving and leaving.

Be deliberate. Think through the role the pastor and family have had in your life: Where have you grown, been challenged? How has God changed you as a result of your time together? As Linda Edelstein said, "Mourning is . . . a process of remembering all the loveliness in life and in ourselves."[1] With deliberate thought we can turn a leaving into a celebration.

Be real. Don't say something you don't mean or act in a way that is not congruous with your character. If you are not a hug-ger, shake a hand warmly and say what you want and need to say. Write a note, make a pie; whatever is in your nature is the way to effect closure in this relationship.

FILL IN THE BLANKS
(When you don't know what to say)

■ I'll miss you. You have touched me in this way . . .

■ Here is what you have meant to me/us . . .

■ I'm sorry for . . .

■ How are you feeling about the move?

■ What troubles you most about the move?

■ What will you miss the most?

Being real includes telling the truth. In one church, a person behind a tidal wave of conflict that resulted in the pastor's forced departure stood in the receiving line. Offering a handshake, the parishioner said, "We'll sure miss you, Pastor." The seasoned pastor met the other's eyes frankly, knowing full well the person's role in the fracas. Perhaps truth in this instance would have been for the parishioner to skip the line altogether.

Being real applies to clergy too. In a Missouri church, the denomination asked the pastor to take another charge. While "no" would have been an acceptable response, the minister told the congregation the change was mandatory. This left church members angry about the untimely move, which prohibited full and cleansing grief over the pastor's leaving. The incoming pastor, who in the congregation's eyes also represented the denomination, became the target for their unexpressed hostility. All this could have been averted, and the work of God not delayed or destroyed, if the outgoing pastor had been honest: "I have been asked to take the next church, and while I could have said no, I accepted. I will miss you, we have done good work together, but this feels like the next likely stop in the sojourn of ministry."

Be expressive. Don't be afraid of emotions. Glad, mad, sad— these three sum up the possibilities in our emotional range.

Sharing them, even with tears, is good. Some of us are afraid that if we cry the dam will burst and we will never stop, or that hysteria will loom, or we'll plunge into depression, or we'll just look stupid or ugly or undignified. Who cares? People need to know they are valued and loved, and that only happens by showing our feelings. Then we can seek times and places for communicating gratitude to the minister and family.

FOR THE PASTOR
1. How could you help the congregation create closure for your relationship?
2. When have you been less deliberate or real with your people?
3. What parting gifts would you like to give the church? What blessing?

And Don't Forget the Pastor's Children
Moving is not just hard on the minister. The spouse and children feel the same emotional spectrum; after a move their identities have to be re-established, their niches carved anew. The disruption in a child's life in particular is immense, with all sense of structure and familiarity ripped away. Abject loneliness after a move, the abyss of knowing no one, realizing that the friends left behind will go on without you—it's a heartbreaking process for children. And terribly difficult for parents to watch.

Talk to the children about the move. Be positive, but leave room for them to express feelings. "It will be different and hard at times, but you can do it. And every time I think of you, I will pray for you. And God will go with you too."

And create a special memory. For example, you could buy an autographable something for the child. Have special friends— the children's choir or Sunday school or youth group—sign it. I found a little stuffed dog covered with five-year-olds' signatures belonging to our fifteen-year-old from a move in kindergarten. I can still see our child embracing the keepsake.

Creating Opportunities for Closure

Closure doesn't happen magically. It takes conscious effort on all parts. The men's group, women's group, Sunday school class, choir—circles of involvement and belonging are important places for celebrating a pastor's gifts, friendship and involvement. A special luncheon or breakfast, a going-away shower, a small-group dessert night, even a packing powwow—anything is possible. Don't overlook a staff goodbye party and prayer time, or an "Elders' and Pastor" meal. Provide a structured question like, "My favorite memory of the pastor is . . . " or "The thing I will miss most about you is . . . " or "God blew me away when this happened . . . "

Expect pain to surface. As we left one church where I had been deeply involved in various arenas, I attended several goodbye events. At each one, my heart felt as if it were being run through a shredder as we remembered and laughed and cried and prayed. But after the move the grief ran its circuit cleanly and lasted less time than in any other move.

FOR THE PASTOR
1. How do you best do your grieving?
2. Can you help family members maintain stability and consistency with each other and with God?
3. What about your own spiritual structure during the throes of moving?

An official going-away service and reception are important gifts to both clergy and congregation. Once the pianist with whom I had led a hymn-sing planned all the music for our last Sunday together. As the notes rolled off the piano, memories welled up in my soul. She had chosen our favorite hymns to sing either in the opening time or during the service itself. If you know some of the favorites, you might include them in the closing worship.

Invite the pastor and family, if appropriate, to be involved in spots where their gifts could bless others one last time. In one church, the people orchestrated the reception and we concentrated on the worship service. There, all five in our family participated in worship—reading liturgy and Scripture, singing, playing instruments. It was good to love the congregation as a unit one last time and be loved in return.

The farewell reception needs forethought—and food if it's held after the service! Don't be afraid to plan for emotions— this is about corporate grief and joyful celebration. Provide people with time to share God's movement in hearts and lives during the pastor's ministry. You might consider asking people in advance to share specific memories to get things started— maybe from the staff or a small group the pastor or a family member is in. Be sure people can be heard—a roving microphone is less threatening than a stationary mike, which may feel too official. Special solos, readings, tributes, jokes, funny stories, "I remember when" tales, going away letters and mementos, a special gift—all are possibilities for the departure party. (For more ideas, see appendix G, "So Long, Farewell.")

A Celebration

Goodbyes are inevitable—but great goodbyes are invaluable. The years together as pastor and church are years of seesaw emotions, change, occasional conflict and deep bonding. This partnership has been through trauma and triumph, gore and glory—and ultimately served together to build God's kingdom on earth. It is miraculous that God takes our lives and brings people to Christ through us, fallible and broken as we are; that we are one body, many gifts, serving together. The church that Jesus established two thousand years ago continues to flourish in our midst! This is a celebration!

We've come through dangers, toils and snares in our church. And when we've been there ten thousand years—bright shining as the sun—we've no less days to sing God's praise. We have made mistakes and learned to love one another well and will sing together again in glory. So let's start right now, singing praise for the amazing grace that brings us together and binds us into a community and sends us out to spread that grace.

Let's make this goodbye great. Not only do you send your pastor on to the next church as your emissary, but when the trumpet sounds one last time, we'll be saying "Hello!" once again.

Loving the Pastor We Have Kept

The hardest thing about moving for me personally is _____ _____. Do my pastor and family feel the same? How can I help with that feeling or issue?

What is the worst thing that would happen if I grieved openly during this transition time for our church, our pastor, myself?

What is my greatest regret during this pastor's tenure? How can I find grace for that regret and express it to the pastor or family member?

And the greatest joys: I have seen God do many things in this church and in my heart. I will celebrate these things with the pastoral family by:

How can I help the pastor's spouse or children in this strange transition time?

Here is how I will pray for my pastor and family as they move:

Appendix A

How to Pray for Your Pastor

The following passages contain New Testament writers' cries for specific prayer from the people. As with any Scripture, it is good to read a verse in context; read the verses surrounding the excerpt below—the writers' faith, peril, need and contentment in Christ are amazing. For instance, in the first selection, Paul asks them to pray that he be rescued from unbelievers and that his service be acceptable to the saints.

Romans 15:30: "I urge you, brothers, by our Lord Jesus Christ and by the love of the Spirit, to join me in my struggle by praying to God for me."

Ephesians 6:19-20: "Pray also for me, that whenever I open my mouth, words may be given me so that I will fearlessly make known the mystery of the gospel. . . . Pray that I may declare it fearlessly, as I should." (This follows right on the heels of the passage about putting on the whole armor of God! Paul needed the same message. So does your pastor.)

Philippians 1:19: "I know that through your prayers and the help given by the Spirit of Jesus Christ, what has happened to me will turn out for my deliverance." (Note the equality linking the prayers of Christians in Philippi with the help given by the Holy Spirit.)

Colossians 4:3-4: "Pray for us, too, that God may open a door for our message, so that we may proclaim the mystery of Christ. . . . Pray that I may proclaim it clearly, as I should." (This is mentioned in the same breath as "devote yourselves to prayer." Their personal discipline of prayer and their prayers for Paul were linked together. Together they forward the gospel!)

1 Thessalonians 1:2-3: "We always thank God for all of you, mentioning you in our prayers. We continually remember before our God and Father your work produced by faith, your labor prompted by love, and your endurance inspired by hope in our Lord Jesus Christ."

1 Thessalonians 5:25: "Pray for us."

2 Thessalonians 3:1-2: "Pray for us that the message of the Lord may spread rapidly and be honored, just as it was with you. And pray that we may be delivered from wicked and evil men, for not everyone has faith."

Hebrews 13:18-19: "Pray for us. We are sure that we have a clear conscience and desire to live honorably in every way. I particularly urge you to pray so that I may be restored to you soon." (Notice the writer's longing for fellowship.)

More Prayer Power

Stumped on how to pray specifically for your pastor? In addition to getting a list of specific prayer concerns, try praying some of the great prayers of the Scriptures. You might even write out your prayers for your clergy as you meditate on the following verses; then mail the prayers to your minister.

John 17	Colossians 1:9-12
Ephesians 1:16-23	2 Thessalonians 2:16-17
Ephesians 3:16-21	2 Thessalonians 1:11-12
Philippians 1:9-11	2 Thessalonians 2:16-17
Colossians 1:3-6	

Appendix B

Bible Study on Loving Your Pastor

Here are some texts and reflection questions for small group or individual study.

John 15:17: Given the major areas of concern for clergy, how can I love my pastor concretely?

Romans 12:10: What does it look like to be devoted to and honor my pastor?

Romans 14:19: How can I build up my minister and staff?

Romans 15:5: What does it mean to be of the same mind as my pastor?

Romans 15:7: In what areas do I need to accept my minister? Where am I struggling to do so? Why?

Romans 15:14: Instruction involves giving earnest advice or encouragement to someone. Note the precedent: first the instructor is to be "full of goodness." Only then do we consider giving gentle, friendly reproof.

Galatians 5:13: How can I serve the pastor through love? How has the pastor exemplified service for me?

Galatians 6:2: What burdens are my clergy carrying? How can I get to know those burdens and then act to relieve them?

Ephesians 4:32: Kind, tenderhearted, forgiving: where have I failed to fulfill this Scripture in the life of my shepherd? Name one way to implement each characteristic.

1 Thessalonians 5:11: Edify, encourage, build up: powerful words with life-changing effects that your pastor desperately needs. Brainstorm ways to do all three.

1 Peter 4:9: When did I last show hospitality to my clergy family?

1 Peter 4:10: What gifts have I received? How can I use them to serve the minister?

Appendix C

Sabbaticals & Renewal Leaves

In the seventh year the land is to have a sabbath of rest,
a sabbath to the LORD. Do not sow your fields or prune your vineyards.
Do not reap what grows of itself or harvest the grapes of your untended vines.
The land is to have a year of rest.

L E V I T I C U S   2 5 : 4 - 5

What a Sabbatical Is

☐ Separate from vacation

☐ Two months to a year for rest, renewal, study, travel

☐ Typically two to six months are with pay; negotiable for remainder of time

☐ Place/time for grounding in deep biblical truth

☐ Place for perspective and reprogramming balance between work, rest, relationships

☐ Typically must include board-approved study and travel plans and report to governing board on return with the results of the leave

☐ Church provides funding for pulpit supply, interim pastor

☐ Minister agrees to stay at current church for another year following return

What a Sabbatical Isn't
☐ Not good for burnout recovery
☐ Not a holiday or vacation
☐ Not a time to do intensive course work
☐ Not a fix for distressed clergy

Variations
☐ Renewal leave three to four months with pay, every four years
☐ Spiritual growth and continuing education week with pay yearly

Watch Out for
☐ Too-high expectations of sabbatical
☐ Over-scheduling during time of renewal
☐ Church staff who insist on contact/approval during leave
☐ Pastors who can't let go while gone and are always checking in
☐ Considering this a fix for a minister in crisis

Good Ideas
☐ Gift collection to send them on their way
☐ Special trip in midst of sabbatical as gift
☐ Give the pastor a trip plus a laptop computer
☐ Write into job description/contract regular renewal and sabbatical leaves
☐ Check endowments and grants for funding in addition to regular local church salary[1]

Ask, What does it take to renew someone as a person so they can be revitalized? Sabbaticals do not need to be functional (e.g., go study something in order to implement a new mission in the church).

> Congregational leaders need to be able to speak from depth. We are not talking about managing or running an institution. How do you offer the perspective that comes from the deep truth of the gospel? Pastors must be well-grounded, have a spiritual/biblical foundation and be well-balanced in their lives. Sabbaticals make that possible. (from a conversation with Gil Rendal, The Alban Institute)

For further reference, see A. Richard Bullock and Richard J. Bruese-hoff, *Clergy Renewal: The Alban Guide to Sabbatical Planning* (Washington, D.C.: Alban Institute, 2000).

Appendix D

The Pastor's Bottom Line

Pastor's Bottom Line

Amount of Paycheck (what you see is *more* than what you get)

Add	Housing Allowance
Less	Insurance
Less	Social Security (15.3% of [Paycheck + Housing Allowance])
Less	Federal Taxes (approx. 15% of paycheck)
Less	State Taxes (approx. 9% of paycheck)
Less	Travel
Less	Business & Professional Expenses
Less	Ministry-Related Hospitality/Entertainment

Equals Money to Live On

Employee's Bottom Line

Gross Pay

Add	Non-Cash Benefits:
	Insurance
	Employer's Social Security (7.65% of gross pay)
	Travel
	Business/Professional Expenses
	Continuing Ed.
Less	Social Security (7.65% of gross pay)
Less	Federal Taxes
Less	State Taxes

Take-Home Pay: _____ (The dollar amount on each paycheck. What you see is *less* than what you get.)

Appendix E

Evaluating Burnout

The following questions need about thirty seconds each. Think back over the past six months. Evaluate life at work, socially and at home. Burnout is seen most easily by people around us, so have a friend or family member rate you as well. Rank each answer from 1 (little or no change) to 5 (a great deal of change).

1. Do you tire more easily? Feel fatigued rather than energetic?

   1 2 3 4 5

2. Are people annoying you by telling you, "You don't look too good lately?

   1 2 3 4 5

3. Are you working harder and harder and accomplishing less and less?

   1 2 3 4 5

4. Are you increasingly cynical and disenchanted? 1 2 3 4 5

5. Are you often invaded by a sadness you can't explain?

   1 2 3 4 5

6. Are you forgetting (appointments, deadlines, personal possessions)?

   1 2 3 4 5

7. Are you increasingly irritable? More short-tempered? More disappointed in the people around you? 1 2 3 4 5

8. Are you seeing close friends and family members less frequently?
1 2 3 4 5

9. Are you too busy to do even routine things like make phone calls or read reports or send out your Christmas cards?   1 2 3 4 5

10. Are you suffering from physical complaints (aches, pains, headaches, a lingering cold)?   1 2 3 4 5

11. Do you feel disoriented when the activity of the day comes to a halt?
1 2 3 4 5

12. Is joy elusive?   1 2 3 4 5

13. Are you unable to laugh at a joke about yourself?   1 2 3 4 5

14. Does sex seem like more trouble than it's worth?   1 2 3 4 5

15. Do you have very little to say to people?   1 2 3 4 5

Scoring

0-25	You're doing fine.
26-35	There are things you should be watching.
36-50	You're a candidate for burnout.
51-65	You are burning out.
Over 65	You're in a dangerous place, threatening to your physical and mental well-being.[1]

Appendix F

Housing Help

Sample Parsonage Guidelines

Standard parsonage equipment which churches are expected to furnish:

Stove, gas or electric

Hot water heater, gas or electric

Electric refrigerator

Automatic dishwasher

Automatic washer and dryer

Carpeting in living room, dining room, family room, hall and stairways

Window coverings (shades/blinds/curtains/draperies) throughout the house

Water softener, where hardness of water indicates need

Kitchen with ample cabinets, counter space, good lighting, adequate electrical wiring for modern appliances, durable floor covering and place for family to eat

Garbage disposal desirable (except with septic systems)

Air conditioner/conditioning—desirable

Sufficient insulation/storm doors/windows to insure home warmth

and efficiency from heating system
Lawn mower, hedge trimmers, snowblower, water hose, if needed
Garbage and recyclable containers appropriate for area
TV antenna or cable hookup if needed
Smoke detectors, fire extinguisher
Exhaust/ventilation system for bathrooms and kitchen
Microwave oven and freezers should be considered
Properly labeled fuse box, ample electrical outlets, all connections
Sump pump where needed to insure a dry basement

Parsonage Space Needs

Garage, double desirable, with ample space for lawn and garden equipment; automatic door opener helpful
Three bedrooms and a guest room or study
Outdoor living space suitable for recreation and beautification with some privacy
A dining room/family room with seating space for eight
Suitably large living room and family or recreation room
Provision for adequate study area
At least two bathrooms
Area for children to play safely outside
Adequate closet and storage space
Most parsonages need at least 2,000 square feet[1]

Move-In Checklist

Organize a food chain for the first week after the move.
Stop by with staples—milk, ice cream, juice, cereal and so on.
Ask for a grocery list and fill it for the new clergy.
Find out what work needs to be done before unpacking: wallpaper hung, a bathroom painted, a fence repaired? Then go to work.
Ask, "Can I unpack and hand you items? Collapse boxes?"
Volunteer to help with heavy furniture.
A welcome pack of picture hangers, mollies, nails, screws and so on would be truly appreciated.

After a week (or three) of settling in, the walls will probably still be bare. With proper tools, offer to help hang pictures and other treasures.

Show up with a lawnmower to help out with maintenance lawn work throughout the throes of unpacking.

One church asked what flowers I wanted for the deck planters and then filled them for me!

When in doubt, *ask* how to help.

Appendix G

So Long, Farewell . . .

Here are some helps for creating going-away celebrations and memories.

Practical Goodbyes
Organize meals (in disposable dishes) for the final week.
Show up at the door and ask, "What can we pack?" Bring boxes, tape, markers, newspaper or wrapping tissue.
Offer to help with small children. Press for a time if the family hesitates to accept.
Bring friends and cleaning supplies and ring the doorbell. "Where should we start?"
Help catch up on mending, alterations, ironing, even laundry during the final week. (I have moved boxes marked "Ironing" and "Mending" only to find them, unopened, when packing for the next move years later!)
Help sort, clean, sharpen, repair tools.
Find out what unfinished home repairs and projects must be completed prior to pulling out, and ask to help with them.
Offer to take blankets, sheets, comforters, towels and curtains to the

laundromat or cleaners several days before moving. You could loan them your own supplies and wash them after they've moved.

Hire a cleaning service to surprise the departing family, saving them the energy of deep cleaning the parsonage after the movers empty it.

Send a "Welcome to Your New Home" card or gift to their new address, so it's there when they arrive.

Pray, pray, pray with them and for them. Pray for safety in travel, energy, recovery from emotional and physical exhaustion, fruit that remains, blessing on the new ministry, healing of grief and loss, and so on.

Scriptures for Comfort in a Move

The LORD himself goes before you and will be with you; he will never leave you nor forsake you. Do not be afraid; do not be discouraged. (Deut 31:8)

Faithful is He who calls you, and He also will bring it to pass. (1 Thess 5:24 NASB)

See, I am sending an angel ahead of you to guard you along the way and to bring you to the place I have prepared. (Ex 23:20)

See, I am doing a new thing! Now it springs up; do you not perceive it? I am making a way in the desert and streams in the wasteland. (Is 43:19)

"For I know the plans I have for you," declares the LORD, "plans to prosper you and not to harm you, plans to give you hope and a future." (Jer 29:11)

In your unfailing love you will lead the people you have redeemed. In your strength you will guide them to your holy dwelling. (Ex 15:13)

Appendix H

Pastoral Care Resources

Leadership and Conflict Consultants
(Programs and training in leadership development and conflict resolution)

Freedom Ministries International
Ardyce Miller, Executive Director
518 North Chelton Road
Suite E
Colorado Springs, CO 80909
Phone: (719) 634-3040
Fax: (719) 634-3374
E-mail: freedom@freedomministries international.org
Web: www.freedomministries international.org
Trains leaders in practical scriptural principles which lead to transformation, restoration and effective ministry.

Injoy, Inc.
John C. Maxwell
P.O. Box 7700
Atlanta, GA 30357
Phone: (800) 333-6506
Fax: (800) 446-0454
Web:www.injoy.com
A nondenominational Christian leadership organization committed to increasing the leadership effectiveness of people in ministry, business and the family through training seminars, books, videos and audiocassettes.

The Leadership Center
David Morgan, Executive Director
Stephen Bravo, Associate Director
P.O. Box 2009
Wolfeboro, NH 03894

Phone:(603) 569-4004
Fax: (603) 569-4773
*Facilities, staff and resources that
provide encouragement to those in
ministry, with a focus on training
church leaders. Includes a pastors and
wives retreat twice a year.*

**Ministering to Ministers
Foundation, Inc.**
Charles Chandler, Executive
 Director
2641 Cromwell Road
Richmond, VA 23235
Phone: (804) 320-6463
Fax: (804) 320-9178
E-mail: mtmfoundation@aol.org
Web: www.bengtson.org/mtm
*Serves to improve church/minister
relations, offers spiritual and emo-
tional support for ministers and their
spouses experiencing involuntary sep-
aration, seeks sources for emergency
funds and provides referrals for career
assessment and placement.*

The Pastoral Institute
Marvin Gardner, Director
3635 Manassas Drive SW, Suite A
Roanoke, VA 24018
Phone: (540) 345-6030
Fax: (540) 345-7415
E-mail: contact@drmarvgardner.com
Web: www.drmarvgardner.com
*Telephone, online or office assis-
tance for pastors caught in church*

*conflict and pastoral families under
antagonist attack.*

Pastors.com
Rick Warren
20131 Ellipse
Foothill Ranch, CA 92610
Phone: (866) 829-0300 (toll-free)
Fax: (949) 829-0400
E-mail: info@pastors.com
Web: www.pastors.com
*A resource ministry for pastors
and church leaders.*

Peacemaker Ministries
Ken Sande, President
1537 Avenue D, Suite 352
Billings, MT 59102
Phone: (406) 256-1583
Fax: (406) 256-0001
E-mail: mail@hispeace.org
Web: www.hispeace.org
*Provides resources, training, con-
flict counseling and mediation/arbi-
tration services to equip and assist
Christians in responding to conflict
biblically.*

**Resources for Resolving Conflict,
 Inc.**
Marlin E. Thomas, President
P.O. Box 724
Milford, NE 68405
Phone: (402) 761-3732
Fax: (402) 761-3732
E-mail: marlin.thomas@rrcinc.org

Web: www.rrcinc.org

A national resource agency for assistance in congregational conflict resolution, seminars for pastors, training of lay leaders, team-building workshops and planning re-treats. Books and cassette tapes also available.

Restored Ministries, Inc.

Al Grounds, Founder/President

Phyllis Grounds, Contact

2025 Harbor Drive

Smyrna, TN 37167

Phone: (615) 459-5360,

  (615) 904-4108

Fax: (615) 459-2234

E-mail: ministryconflict@aol.com

Web: http://river-of-life.net/

ms_grounds.htm

Supports ministers and their families by assisting them in bringing healing to broken congregations.

Reflection and Relaxation Providers

(Locations for unstructured personal reflection and renewal)

Beulah Beach Corp.

Tonya Montgomery, Contact

6101 West Lake Road

Vermilion, OH 44089

Phone: (440) 967-4861

Fax: (440) 967-4783

E-mail: registrations@

beulahbeach.org

Web: www.beulahbeach.org

A place where pastors and their families can be refreshed, restored and revived in the presence of God. Located on the beautiful shores of Lake Erie between Cleveland and Toledo, Ohio.

Camp Berachah Ministries

Steve Altick, Executive Director

19830 SE 328th Place

Auburn, WA 98092

Phone: (253) 939-0488

Fax: (253) 833-7027

E-mail: staff@berachahcamp.org

Web: www.berachahcamp.org

Offers personal retreat time for pastors, their families and others in full-time Christian ministry. Facilities available for church planning. Recreation available as well as space for personal quiet time.

The Escape House

Rob and Debbie Killeffer

192 West Street

Braintree, MA 02184

Phone: (781) 356-8286

E-mail: mrspastor7@aol.com

Web: members.aol.com/mrspastor7

Fully equipped, year-round, quiet country lakeside home in southwest New Hampshire that serves as a vacation or mini-retreat for pastors, missionaries and seminary students.

Faith Mountain Ministries, Inc.
Herb and Kathy Miller, Directors
HC 73 Box 18 C
Rosedale, WV 26636
Phone: (877) 324-8495,
  (304) 364-4019
Fax: (304) 364-4019
E-mail: faithmtn@access
  .mountain.net
Web: www.faithmountain.org
   Two-bedroom cottages on two hundred beautiful wooded acres in the Mountain Lakes region of West Virginia provide an ideal setting for Christian leaders to experience rest, relaxation and spiritual renewal.

Fallen Goose Lodge and Retreat Center
Mollie D. Lesslie
5628 Highway 93 South
Conner, MT 59827
Phone: (406) 821-1552
Fax: (406) 821-3055
E-mail: fallengoose@
  forsuchatimeasthis.org
Web: www.forsuchatimeasthis.org
   A Christian retreat for pastors, missionaries and their families for rest, relaxation, renewal and even play in this twenty-four-acre mountain valley location.

Harvest Prayer Center
Dave and Kim Butts, Founders
Carl and Gayla Royer, Retreat

Directors
11991 E. Davis Avenue
Brazil, IN 47834
Phone: (812) 443-5703
Fax: (812) 443-5505
E-mail: prayercenter@
  harvestprayer.com
Web: www.harvestprayer.com
   A nondenominational ministry providing a place for ministers, missionaries and Christian leaders and their families to come for relaxation, prayer and spiritual renewal.

Makahiki Ministries
Billie Hair, Director
P.O. Box 415
Mariposa, CA 95338
Phone: (209) 966-2988
Fax: (209) 966-2988
E-mail: makahiki@sierratel.com
Web: www.hospitalityhomes.org
   A network of hospitality homes in the United States and abroad for Christian workers seeking spiritual and physical renewal.

The Retreat
Doug and Barbara Puller, Directors
29961 N. Highway 41
Spirit Lake, ID 83869
Phone: (208) 623-4402
Fax: (208) 623-4402
   A place where pastors, missionaries and their families can come to spend time alone with the Lord for

rest, relaxation and spiritual renewal in an isolated, peaceful forest setting.

Sky Ranch
Wendel Weaver, Conference Center
  Manager
24657 CR448
Van, TX 75790
Phone: (800) 962-2267,
  (903) 569-3482
Fax: (903) 569-6357
E-mail: wendelweaver@juno.com
Web: www.skyranch.org
Conference center available for church staff events or a hideaway lodge for pastors and their spouses to get away. Facilities offered free of charge.

Triple Creek Ranch
348 N. Snipe Hollow Road
Elizabeth, IL 61028
Phone: (815) 858-2435
Fax: (815)858-2270
E-mail: Info@triplecreekranch.org
Web: www.triplecreekranch.org
Completely furnished homes on ranches in Colorado and Illinois available free of charge to full-time Christian pastors and missionaries and their families for refreshment and rest.

Rest and Renewal Retreat Centers
(Locations for personal rejuvenation and rest with optional light counseling services)

America's Keswick
Bill Welte, Director
601 Route 530
Whiting, NJ 08759
Phone: (732) 350-1187
Fax: (732) 849-2926
E-mail: keswickexe@aol.com
Web: www.americaskeswick.org
Offering pastors and spouses rest and relaxation free of charge. A yearly pastors' conference and counseling is also available.

Cedarly Pastors Retreat
Peter Giersch, Executive
  Director
Dwayne and Rita Hanon,
  Senior Host Couple
2841 Mill Road
Oconomowoc, WI 53066
Phone: (262) 646-7772
Fax: (262) 646-7773
E-mail: cedarly@execpc.com
Web: www.cedarly.org
Secluded country retreats in Wisconsin, Michigan and Texas that provide an environment for prayer, reflection and fellowship to refocus one's commitment and relationship to God and spouse. Self-directed programs; no counseling.

Mountain Top Retreat
Harold and Beulah Erickson,
  Founders
Len Bauer, Administrator

13705 Cottonwood Canyon Rd.
Bozeman, MT 59718
Phone: (406) 763-4566
Fax: (406) 763-4566
E-mail: mtroffice@mcn.net
Web: www.mountaintopretreat.org

A quiet, private mountain setting for pastors, missionaries and their families to find rest and renewal. Light counseling provided.

SonScape Re-Creation Ministries

Bob Sewell, Director
Roy Fitzwater, Contact
P.O. Box 7777
Woodland Park, CO 80866
Phone: (888) 766-7227,
   (719) 687-7007
Fax: (719) 687-7877
E-mail: sonscape@usa.net
Web: www.sonscape.com

Small-group (four couples or three couples and an unmarried single), eight-day spiritual formation retreat for those in professional Christian ministry. Provides private cottages with fireplaces and hot tubs, gourmet meals, daily devotions, teaching and personal counseling for life, marriage and ministry. (No children.)

Restoration and Counseling Retreat Centers

(Retreat facilities for restoration through intensive counseling)

Alongside, Inc. at Tuscarora Resource Center

Jeanne J. Jensma, Director of Counseling
P.O. Box 587
Richland, MI 49083-0587
Phone: (616) 671-4809
E-mail: info@alongsidecares.org
Web: www.alongsidecares.org

Provides professional, spiritual, mental and emotional caregiving services to people in Christian ministry and their families, including a two-and-a-half-week retreat offered monthly on the grounds of a nearby conference center or staff travel to other sites.

Charis Counseling Services (East)

Frank Green
7716 Fallbranch Court
Wake Forest, NC 27587
Phone: (919) 556-1887,
   (919) 244-8213
E-mail: charis@teleport.com
Web: www.teleport.com/~charis

An organization committed to bringing healing and renewal to the lives of Christian leaders through two-week retreat programs of individual, couple or group counseling.

Charis Counseling Services (West)

Larry Barber
559 River Loop #1
Eugene, OR 97404

Phone: (541) 607-0601
E-mail: charis@teleport.com
Web: www.teleport.com/~charis
*An organization committed to
bringing healing and renewal to the
lives of Christian leaders through
two-week retreat programs of individual, couple or group counseling.*

The Dove Center
Michael L. Hill, Executive
  Director
Sharon P. Hill, Director of Training
  & Psychotherapy
14520 Perdido Key Drive
Pensacola, FL 32507
Phone: (850) 492-3683,
  (877) 238-6664
Fax: (850) 497-8044
E-mail: info@thedovecenter.org
Web: www.thedovecenter.org
*Professionally licensed counseling
services and pastoral care in a beach-
front resort location.*

Eagles Nest Retreat
John Gowins, Executive
  Director
P.O. Box 1165
Ouray, CO 81427
Phone: (800) 533-4049
E-mail: enretreat@aol.com
*A sanctuary of rest, recreation and
restoration providing either profes-
sional counseling or unstructured
vacation.*

Fairhaven Ministries
Kevin and Linda Swanson, Directors
2198 Roaring Creek Road
Roan Mountain, TN 37687
Phone: (423) 772-4269
Fax: (423) 772-0017
E-mail: fhmin@aol.com
Web: www.fairhaven1.com
*Rest, recreation and renewal are
offered in beautiful chalets in the
Great Smoky Mountains through
vacations, personal retreats or profes-
sional counseling. Ministry marriage
retreats are offered in the winter
months.*

Gray Fox Ranch
Walter and Françoise Becker,
  Directors
P.O. Box 434
Alto, NM 88312
Phone: (877) 472-9333
Fax: (505) 336-9126
E-mail: waltbecker@aol.com
Web: www.grayfox.org
*A private marital retreat with a
special program for pastors providing
intensive counseling toward restora-
tion.*

His High Places, Inc.
Sam McMillan, Director
Anita McMillan, Contact
P.O. Box 1615
701 Berry Road
Banner Elk, NC 28604

Phone: (828) 963-4866
Fax: (828) 963-6840
E-mail: hishighplace@
  skybest.com
Web: www.hishighplaces.org
  Provides a week of in-residence
experience in one of God's most pic-
turesque mountain settings, led by
licensed professional counselors who
have previously served many years in
pastoral ministry.

The Lamb's Tale
Dr. John Ramsey, Dr. Suzanne
  Ellison
200 W. Windcrest, Ste. 200
Fredericksburg, TX 78624
Phone: (830) 990-1475
Web: www.christian-retreats.com
  Offering counseling and retreats to
people in ministry as well as other
organizations; a restored country inn
on the Guadeloupe River; licensed
professional counselors; high teas,
exquisite food and the comforting
presence of God.

Leadership Renewal Center, Inc.
Ted and Linda Pampeyan
4964 Georgia Park Terrace
Victoria, BC V8Y 2B9
Phone: (250) 658-8510
Fax: (250) 658-8561
E-mail: leadershiprenewal@
  shaw.ca
Web: www.leadershiprenewal.com

A four-day private retreat in a
B&B ocean-view setting for the pastoral couple's spiritual and ministry
career renewal, offering personal and
professional counseling, private bed-
room suite, gourmet meals and dinner
cruise.

Marble Retreat
Louis and Melissa McBurney,
  Founders/Therapists
Cheryl Yarrow, Executive Director
139 Bannockburn
Marble, CO 81623
Phone: (888) 216-2725,
  (970) 963-2499
Fax: (970) 963-0217
E-mail: mretreat@compuserve.com
Web: www.marbleretreat.org
  An interdenominational crisis
counseling retreat center providing
care since 1974 for those in Christian
ministry. Group and individual coun-
seling by a board-certified psychiatrist
or a licensed therapist offered in
twelve-day intensive sessions.

The Marriage Retreat
Forrest Mobley, Executive Director
4421 Commons Drive E PMB 404
Destin, FL 32541
Phone: (850) 650-8000
Fax: (850) 650-8001
  Individualized seven-day pro-
grams of teaching and counseling to
refresh and renew marriages.

Mountain Learning Center
Russell R. Veenker, Pastoral
  Counselor
Kandy Veenker, Executive Director
P.O. Box 625
June Lake, CA 93529
Phone: (800) 293-2508,
  (760) 648-7060
Fax: (760) 648-7867
E-mail: pastorcare@qnet.com
Web: www.pastor-care.com
  A two-week retreat for pastors and their spouses designed to revitalize their relationship with God and others through physically, emotionally and spiritually invigorating experiences.

Northwest Family Ministries
Peter J. DePaoli, Executive
  Director
17935 SW Alexander
P.O. Box 5104
Aloha, OR 97006
Phone: (503) 356-0456
Web: www.nwfm.org
  Provides ongoing daily ministry to pastors and their families using biblically based tools to promote emotional, interpersonal and spiritual healing. Cosponsors retreats with conference centers.

**Oasis Retreats (Campus
Crusade for Christ)**
Pete & Shirley Unrau, Retreat
  Directors

P.O. Box 300 Station A
Vancouver, BC V6C 2X3
Phone: (800) 563-1106,
  (604) 850-8795
Fax: (604) 514-2124
E-mail: punrau@direct.ca
Web: www.crusade.org/oasis
  Provides a number of small five-day retreats at Cedar Springs Retreat Center in Sumas, Washington, annually that will refresh and restore those wounded and weary in ministry.

Paraklesis Ministries
Sidney Draayer, Director
1550 E. Beltline SE, Suite 360
Grand Rapids, MI 49506
Phone: (800) 421-8352,
  (616) 957-9709
Fax: (616) 957-1699
E-mail: info@paraklesis.org
Web: www.paraklesis.org
  Helps pastors and their spouses grow spiritually, emotionally and relationally through counseling, seminars, consultations and retreats.

Restoration House
Daniel L. Garvin
545 N. Glassy Mountain Road
Landrum, SC 29356
Phone: (864) 977-8020
  A place where missionaries, pastors and Christian leaders can come to receive healing from deep emotional wounds and personal struggles.

Restoration Ministries
Steve Fetrow, Director/Counselor
1526 E. Harry St.
Wichita, KS 67211
Phone: (316) 263-1276
Fax: (316) 263-2899
E-mail: DrFetrow@
woodlandlakescc.com
Web: www.woodlandlakescc.com/
restoration
Offers an eight-day Critical Concentrated Counseling program for
pastors, Christian leaders and families. Special emphasis is placed on the
restoration process and recovery from
sexual addiction.

Stone Gate Resources
Harry W. Schaumburg, Executive
Director
11509 Palmer Divide Road
Larkspur, CO 80118
Phone: (303) 688-5680,
  (888) 575-3030
Fax: (303) 688-5938
E-mail: stonegater@cs.com
Web: www.stonegateresources.org
A secluded retreat setting with
lodging and meals that provides per-
sonal restoration through ten days of
intensive counseling.

Westwood Ministries
Dave T. Gentry, Executive Director
P.O. Box 291446
Kerrville, TX 78029

Phone: (800) 583-9841,
  (830) 634-3082
Fax: (830) 634-7001
E-mail: westwood@ktc.com
Web: www.westwoodministries.org
An interdenominational ministry
dedicated to the health and healing of
Christian leaders and their families.
Ministries include counseling, men-
toring, sabbatical/retreat, life/minis-
try training and church consulting.

Miscellaneous Ministries
(A variety of services and unique ministries)

Barnabas International
Lareau Lindquist, Executive Direc-
tor
P.O. Box 11211
Rockford, IL 61126
Phone: (815) 395-1335
Fax: (815) 395-1385
E-mail: barnabas@barnabas.org
Web: www.barnabas.org
A ministry to missionaries and
nationals in church leadership con-
sisting of individual and team coun-
seling, consultation, retreats and
conferences.

Barnabas Ministries
Richard Sochacki, Director
39391 Roslyn Drive
Sterling Heights, MI 48313
Phone: (810) 264-6638

E-mail: rlsochacki@cs.com

*Encourages and strengthens
ministers through workshops,
seminars, personal counseling,
ministry networking and
resources.*

Biblical Wellness Ministries
Bill Reynolds, President
5102A Oak Park Road
Raleigh, NC 27612
Phone: (919) 783-6075
Fax: (919) 783-0655
E-mail: biblicalwm@aol.com

*A renewal ministry of retreats,
counseling, mediation/conflict
management and financial
counseling to pastors, church
officers, Christian workers and
their families.*

Elijah's Brook
David Rogenes, Director
P.O. Box 447
Glasgow, MT 59230
Phone: (406) 228-2694
Fax: (406) 228-9554
E-mail: glasgowag@juno.com

*A residential facility for pastors in
transition.*

**Pastoral Ministries (Focus on the
Family)**
H. B. London Jr., Vice President
Colorado Springs, CO 80995-7001
Phone: (877) 233-4455,

(719) 531-3360
Fax: (719) 531-3347
Web: www.parsonage.org

*Consultation, resources and
referrals for pastors, spouses and their
families, including a toll-free pastoral
care line (listed above).*

PastorCare
Filbert L. Moore Jr., Director
P.O. Box 52044
Raleigh, NC 27612
Phone: (919) 787-7024
Fax:(919) 571-9878
E-mail: staff@pastorcare.org
Web: www.pastorcare.org

*A national support network that
connects needy pastors and spouses to
support people in seven basic areas:
confidential prayer intercessors,
hospitality hosts for free getaways,
interim employment, lawyers, dentists, physicians, and counselors and
mentors.*

PastorsNet
Dennis Worden, Director
John Maxwell, Founder
P.O. Box 7700
Atlanta, GA 30357
Phone: (770) 239-5222
Fax: (770) 239-5196
E-mail: dennis@injoy.com
Web: www.pastorsnet.org

*A ministry linking pastors with
prayer partners and caregivers.*

Power
Dolores Feitl, Founder and Director
30990 Lexington Way
Westlake Village, CA 91361
Phone: (818) 707-2251
Fax: (818) 735-0748
E-mail: powerfulties@aol.com

Web: http://members.aol.com/dfeitl/power.html

An understanding network of pastors' wives holding an annual retreat, half-day seminars and coordinating local support groups of pastors' wives.

Notes

Chapter 1: A New Definition for "Pastoral Care"

[1]*Focus on the Family Magazine,* September 1994, p. 10.

[2]Dale Schafler, *Seven Promises of a Promise Keeper* (Colorado Springs: Focus on the Family/Word, 1994), p. 136.

[3]*Southern Baptist Convention Newspaper,* December 1990.

[4]Charles Willis, "Lifeway Executive Addresses Churches' 'Dirty Little Secret,'" BPNews (May 5, 1999), as cited in <www.BPNews.net>.

[5]George Barna, *Today's Pastors* (Ventura, Calif.: Regal, 1993), p. 37.

[6]Gary L. McIntosh, "Is It Time to Leave?" *Leadership* (summer 1988), pp. 70-75.

[7]Thom Rainer, *Effective Evangelistic Churches* (Nashville: Broadman & Holman, 1996), pp. 43-44, as quoted in Gary L. McIntosh and Robert L. Edmondson, *It Only Hurts on Monday* (Carol Stream, Ill.: ChurchSmart Resources, 1998), p. 6. George Barna reports that clergy move every four years, down from seven in the last two decades (*Today's Pastors,* p. 36).

[8]Liz Greenbacker and Sherry Taylor, *Private Lives of Ministers' Wives* (Far Hills, N.J.: New Horizons, 1991), p. 228.

[9]H. B. London Jr. and Neil B. Wiseman, *Pastors at Risk* (Wheaton, Ill.: Victor, 1993), p. 22.

[10]*Focus on the Family Magazine,* September 1994, p. 10.

[11]William H. Willimon, *Clergy and Laity Burnout* (Nashville: Abingdon, 1989), p. 78.

[12]Roy M. Oswald, *Clergy Self-Care: Finding a Balance for Effective Ministry* (Washington, D.C.: Alban Institute, 1991), p. xi.

[13]Greenbacker and Taylor, *Private Lives,* p. 228.

Chapter 2: The Welcome Mat

[1]Kathy Leithner, "Moving Day," *Leland Clegg United Methodist Church Newsletter* (Oklahoma City), June 1989, p. 1.

[2]For a more in-depth discussion of loss, please refer to *Quiet Places: A Woman's Guide to Personal Retreat* (Minneapolis: Bethany House, 1997).

[3]Leithner, "Moving Day," p. 1.

[4]Oswald, *Clergy Self-Care*, p. 45.

[5]H. B. London Jr. and Neil B. Wiseman, *They Call Me Pastor: How to Love the Ones You Lead* (Ventura, Calif.: Regal, 2000), p. 142.

[6]Dean Merrill, *Clergy Couples in Crisis* (Dallas: Word/Leadership Books, 1985), p. 80.

[7]Karen Mains, *Friends and Strangers: Divine Encounters in Lonely Places* (Dallas: Word, 1990), p. 23.

Chapter 3: Communication in the Church

[1]H. B. London Jr., speaking in Toronto, Canada, The Age Wave Conference, March 2001.

[2]Gary L. McIntosh and Robert L. Edmondson, *It Only Hurts on Monday: Why Pastors Quit and What You Can Do About It* (Carol Stream, Ill.: ChurchSmart Resources, 1998), p. 171.

[3]H. B. London Jr., speaking in Naperville, Illinois, to a clergy gathering, April 1999.

[4]James H. Strong, *Strong's Concordance* (Nashville: Thomas Nelson, 1997).

[5]"Pastoral Compensation Hits Record Level," March 29, 2001 <www.Barna.org/cgi-bin/PagePressRelease.asp?PressReleaseID=85&Reference=B>.

[6]For a deeper look at staff relationships, see Terry Nance, *God's Armor Bearer: How to Serve God's Leaders* (Tulsa, Okla.: Harrison House, 1990).

[7]BPNews, May 5, 1999, p. 1.

Chapter 4: Beyond the Sunday Sermon

[1]George Barna, *Today's Pastors* (Ventura, Calif.: Regal, 1993), p. 59.

[2]Ibid.

[3]Barbara G. Gilbert, *Who Ministers to Ministers? A Study of Support Systems for Clergy and Spouses* (Washington, D.C.: Alban Institute, 1987), appendix 6.

[4]Ibid., appendix 4.

[5]Stefan Ulstein, *Pastors Off the Record: Straight Talk About Life in the Ministry* (Downers Grove, Ill.: InterVarsity Press, 1993), p. 19.

[6]Barna, *Today's Pastors*, p. 73.

[7]Roy Oswald, *Clergy Self-Care: Finding a Balance for Effective Ministry* (Washington, D.C.: Alban Institute, 1991), p. 95.

[8]E. M. Bounds, *Power Through Prayer* (Grand Rapids, Mich.: Zondervan, 1979), p. 27, as quoted by Richard Foster in *Prayer: Finding the Heart's True Home* (New York: HarperCollins, 1992), p. 115.

[9]Liz Greenbacker and Sherry Taylor, *Private Lives of Ministers' Wives* (Far Hills, N.J.: New Horizons, 1991), p. 228.

[10]Barna, *Today's Pastors*, p. 59.

[11]William H. Willimon, *Clergy and Laity Burnout* (Nashville: Abingdon, 1989), p. 32.

[12]Barna, *Today's Pastors*, pp. 129, 131.

[13]Ibid., p. 49.

Chapter 5: Stress and Burnout

[1]H. B. London Jr. and Neil B. Wiseman, *Pastors at Risk* (Wheaton, Ill.: Victor, 1993), p. 161.

[2]Ibid., pp. 162-63.

[3]James Dobson et al., "How to Beat Burnout," Focus on the Family CS315, 1987, audiocassette.

[4]Roy Oswald, *Clergy Self-Care: Finding a Balance for Effective Ministry* (Washington, D.C.: Alban Institute, 1991), p. 123.

[5]As quoted in a telephone conversation with Dr. Howard Hendricks's office personnel at Dallas Theological Seminary, May 23, 1996.

[6]Barbara G. Gilbert, *Who Ministers to Ministers? A Study of Support Systems for Clergy and Spouses* (Washington, D.C.: Alban Institute, 1987), appendixes 6, 7.

[7]Oswald, *Clergy Self-Care*, p. 130.

[8]Quoted in Douglas J. Brower, comp., *The Pastor's Appreciation Book of Wit and Wisdom* (Wheaton, Ill.: Harold Shaw, 1992), p. 8.

Chapter 6: Single Clergy

[1]George Barna, "Pastoral Compensation Hits Record Level," March 29, 2001 <www.Barna.org/cgi-bin/PagePressRelease.asp?PressReleaseID=85&Reference=B>.

Chapter 7: Paragon of the Pews

[1]Barbara G. Gilbert, *Who Ministers to Ministers?* (Washington, D.C.: Alban Institute, 1987), appendix 8.

[2]H. B. London Jr. and Neil Wiseman, *Pastors at Risk* (Wheaton, Ill.: Victor, 1993), p. 22, quoting Fuller Institute of Church Growth 1991 survey of pastors (Pasadena, Calif.: Fuller Theological Seminary, 1991).

[3]Roy M. Oswald, "Why Do Clergy Wives Burn Out?" *Action Information,* January-February 1984, pp. 11-15.

[4]Barna Research reports that 95 percent of clergy are male; 94 percent are married (March 29, 2001) <www.barna.org>; 1994 figures from Hartford Seminary, when tabulated, point to 8.77 percent of clergy as female <www.hartsem.edu/research/quick_question3.html>.

[5]As cited by Gail MacDonald in *High Call, High Privilege* (Peabody, Mass.: Hendrickson, 1998), p. 50.

[6]Liz Greenbacker and Sherry Taylor, *Private Lives of Ministers' Wives* (Far Hills, N.J.: New Horizons, 1991), p. 76.

[7]Oswald, "Why Do Clergy Wives Burn Out?" pp. 11-15.

[8]Survey results vary. Greenbacker and Taylor report in *Private Lives* that 76 percent of their respondents work outside the home (p. 321). The National Association of Evangelicals cites a 60 percent outside employment rate of ministry wives (February 1990).

[9]Lynne Dugan, *Heart to Heart with Pastors' Wives* (Ventura, Calif.: Regal, 1994), and Kenneth E. Crow, *A Survey of Ministers' Wives* (Wheaton, Ill.: National Association of Evangelicals, 1990), p. 163.

[10]As cited by H. B. London Jr. and Neil Wiseman, *Married to a Pastor's Wife* (Wheaton, Ill.: Victor, 1995), p. 134, quoting Alan B. Mangum's unpublished manuscript *Ministers' Wives Speak Out,* p. 6.

[11]London and Wiseman, *Married to a Pastor's Wife,* p. 284.

[12]Gilbert, *Who Ministers to Ministers?* appendix 5.

[13]Ibid., p. 103, citing data from Kenneth E. Crow, *A Survey of Ministers' Wives* (Wheaton, Ill.: National Association of Evangelicals, 1990).

[14]If you are a hungry soul and would like information about a (mostly) distance mentoring program available through Mainstay Ministries in conjunction with Jane Rubietta, please visit <www.hungrysouls.org> or call 1-800-224-2735.

Chapter 8: Creating a Place for the Children
[1]George Barna, *Today's Pastors* (Ventura, Calif.: Regal, 1993), p. 62.
[2]H. B. London Jr. and Neil Wiseman, *Pastors at Risk* (Wheaton, Ill.: Victor, 1993), p. 30.
[3]"Giving Credit to Our Clergy," *The Saturday Evening Post*, September-October 1996, p. 72, quoting Jerry Frear, director, Under His Wings Ministries.
[4]For more on boundaries, see Jane Rubietta, *Quiet Places: A Woman's Guide to Personal Retreat* (Minneapolis: Bethany House, 1997).
[5]Fuller Institute of Church Growth 1991 survey of pastors (Pasadena, Calif.: Fuller Theological Seminary, 1991).
[6]David Goetz, "Is the Pastor's Family Safe at Home?" *Leadership*, fall 1992, p. 39.
[7]Dean Merrill, *Clergy Couples in Crisis* (Dallas: Word/Leadership Books, 1985), p. 137

Chapter 9: Ministry and Church Accountability
[1]James Dobson, *Family News from Dr. James Dobson*, August 1998, p. 2.
[2]Assimilated from Gail MacDonald, *High Call, High Privilege* (Peabody, Mass.: Hendrickson, 1998), pp. 163-77. Headers are Gail's, descriptions mine.
[3]From Barbara Brown Zikmund, Adair T. Lummis and Patricia M. Y. Chang, *Clergy Women: An Uphill Calling* (Louisville, Ky.: Westminster John Knox, 1998), p. 143, quoted on the Religious Research Page, Hartford Seminary <www.hartsem.edu>.
[4]*Southern Baptist Convention Virginia Newspaper*, December 1990.
[5]H. B. London Jr., presentation at The Age Wave Conference, Toronto, Canada, April 2001.
[6]Archibald Hart, in a taped interview with H. B. London Jr., Pastor to Pastor series, vol. 48, "Dangers of the Internet" (Colorado Springs, Colo.: Focus on the Family, 2000), side 4.
[7]Ibid., side 3.

Chapter 10: Hearth and Home
[1]Liz Greenbacker and Sherry Taylor, *Private Lives of Ministers' Wives* (Far Hills, N.J.: New Horizons, 1991), p. 79.
[2]Author assumes no legal responsibility for financial information in *How to Keep the Pastor You Love*. Please consult a clergy tax or financial adviser before making decisions affecting your church and your ministerial staff.

Chapter 11: When the Ends Don't Meet
[1]Liz Greenbacker and Sherry Taylor, *Private Lives of Ministers' Wives* (Far Hills, N.J.: New Horizons, 1991), p. 77.
[2]George Barna, "Pastoral Compensation Hits Record Level," March 29, 2001 <www.Barna.org/cgi-bin/PagePressRelease.asp?PressReleaseID=85&Reference=B>.
[3]Timothy K. Jones, "How to Keep Your Pastor Happy," *Christianity Today*, September 14, 1992, p. 19.
[4]Gary L. McIntosh and Robert L. Edmondson, *It Only Hurts on Monday* (Carol Stream Ill.: ChurchSmart Resources, 1998), p. 171.
[5]*Leadership*, fall 1992, quoted in H. B. London Jr. and Neil Wiseman, *Pastors at Risk* (Wheaton, Ill.: Victor, 1993), p. 114.
[6]Marshall Shelley, *The Healthy Hectic Home* (Waco, Tex.: Word, 1988), p. 29.
[7]Barbara G. Gilbert, *Who Ministers to Ministers?* (Washington, D.C.: Alban Institute

1987), appendix 8.

[8]Jones, "How to Keep Your Pastor Happy," p. 19.

[9]Greenbacker and Taylor, *Private Lives of Ministers' Wives,* p. 228.

[10]Ibid., p. 76.

[11]Author assumes no legal responsibility for financial information in *How to Keep the Pastor You Love.* Please consult a clergy tax or financial adviser before making decisions affecting your church and your ministerial staff.

Chapter 12: Building Better Clergy Compensation

[1]Based on a quote by a State Farm Insurance agent, September 2001.

[2]The Standing Committee on Clergy Compensation <www.dioceseofnewark.org>.

[3]David L. Goetz, "The Truth about Debt and Salaries," *Leadership,* spring 1997, pp. 85-90.

[4]Based on a conversation with Lonnie Chafin, treasurer, Northern Illinois Conference of the United Methodist Church, September 26, 2001.

Chapter 13: Crisis Care

[1]H. B. London Jr. and Neil Wiseman, *Pastors at Risk* (Wheaton, Ill.: Victor, 1993), p. 163, quoting H. Newton Maloney and Richard A. Hunt, *The Psychology of Clergy* (Harrisburg, Penn.: Morehouse, 1991).

[2]Henri J. M. Nouwen, *Out of Solitude: Three Meditations on the Christian Life* (Notre Dame, Ind.: Ave Maria Press, 1984), pp. 26, 35.

[3]Edgar W. Mills and John P. Koval, *Stress in the Ministry* (Washington, D.C.: Ministry Studies Board, 1971), p. 32.

[4]William H. Willimon, *Clergy and Laity Burnout* (Nashville: Abingdon, 1989), p. 28.

Chapter 14: Great Goodbyes

[1]Linda Edelstein, *The Art of Midlife: Courage and Creativity* (Westport, Conn.: Bergin & Garvey, 1999), p. 21.

Appendix C: Sabbaticals and Renewal Leaves

[1]Lilly Endowment has an official National Clergy Renewal Program; each congregation may request a total of up to $30,000 to support the renewal program of the church/clergy. Write <clergyrenewal@yahoo.com>.

Appendix E: Evaluating Burnout

[1]Herbert J. Freudenberger with Geraldine Richelson, *Burn-Out: The High Cost of High Achievement* (Garden City, N.Y.: Anchor, 1980), pp. 17-18, as quoted by Gary L. McIntosh and Robert L. Edmondson, *It Only Hurts on Monday* (Carol Stream, Ill.: ChurchSmart Resources, 1998), pp. 22-23.

Appendix F: Housing Help

[1]The United Methodist Church, Northern Illinois Conference, Standing Rules (2000), sect. IV-83e, h.

Works Cited

Barna, George. "Pastoral Compensation Hits Record Level." Press release (March 29, 2001) <www.Barna.org/cgi-bin/PagePressRelease.asp?PressReleaseID=85& Reference=B>.

————. *Today's Pastors*. Ventura, Calif.: Regal, 1993.

Bounds, E. M. *Power Through Prayer.* Grand Rapids, Mich.: Zondervan, 1979.

Brower, Douglas J., comp. *The Pastor's Appreciation Book of Wit and Wisdom*. Wheaton, Ill.: Harold Shaw, 1992.

Bubna, Donald L. "How to Bid a Healthy Farewell." *Leadership*, summer 1988.

Bullock, A. Richard, and Richard J. Bruesehoff. *Clergy Renewal: The Alban Guide to Sabbatical Planning*. Washington, D.C.: Alban Institute, 2000.

Dobson, James. *Family News from Dr. James Dobson*, August 1998.

————, et al. "How to Beat Burnout," tape CS315/1090. Colorado Springs: Focus on the Family, 1987, 1994.

Dugan, Lynne. *Heart to Heart with Pastors' Wives*. Ventura, Calif.: Regal, 1994.

Edelstein, Linda. *The Art of Midlife: Courage and Creativity*. Westport, Conn.: Bergin & Garvey, 1999.

Focus on the Family Magazine, September 1994.

Foster, Richard. *Prayer: Finding the Heart's True Home*. New York: HarperCollins, 1992.

Freudenberger, Herbert J., with Geraldine Richelson. *Burn-Out: The High Cost of High Achievement*. Garden City, N.Y.: Anchor, 1980.

Gilbert, Barbara G. *Who Ministers to Ministers? A Study of Support Systems for Clergy and Spouses*. Washington, D.C.: Alban Institute, 1987.

"Giving Credit to Our Clergy." *The Saturday Evening Post,* September-October 1996.

Goetz, David. "Is the Pastor's Family Safe at Home?" *Leadership,* fall 1992.

————. "The Truth About Debt and Salaries." *Leadership,* spring 1997.

Greenbacker, Liz, and Sherry Taylor. *Private Lives of Ministers' Wives*. Far Hills, N.J.: New Horizons, 1991.

Hart, Archibald, M.D., in a taped interview with H. B. London Jr. Pastor to Pastor series, vol. 48, "Dangers of the Internet." Colorado Springs, Colo.: Focus on the Family, 2000.

Jones, Timothy K. "How to Keep Your Pastor Happy." *Christianity Today,* September 14, 1992.

Leithner, Kathy. "Moving Day." *Leland Clegg United Methodist Church* [Oklahoma City] *Newsletter,* June 1989. Poem reprinted with permission of author.

London, H. B., Jr., and Neil Wiseman, *Married to a Pastor's Wife*. Wheaton, Ill.: Victor, 1995.

———. *Pastors at Risk*. Wheaton, Ill.: Victor, 1993.

———. *They Call Me Pastor: How to Love the Ones You Lead*. Ventura, Calif.: Regal, 2000.

MacDonald, Gail. *High Call, High Privilege*. Peabody, Mass.: Hendrickson, 1998.

Mains, Karen. *Friends and Strangers: Divine Encounters in Lonely Places*. Dallas: Word, 1990.

Malony, H. Newton, and Richard A. Hunt. *The Psychology of Clergy*. Harrisburg, Penn.: Morehouse, 1991.

Mangum, Alan B. *Ministers' Wives Speak Out*. Unpublished manuscript.

McIntosh, Gary L. "Is It Time to Leave?" *Leadership* (summer quarter 1988): 70-75.

McIntosh, Gary L., and Robert L. Edmondson. *It Only Hurts on Monday: Why Pastors Quit and What You Can Do About It*. Carol Stream, Ill.: ChurchSmart Resources, 1998.

Merrill, Dean. *Clergy Couples in Crisis*. Dallas: Word/Leadership Books, 1985.

Mills, Edgar W., and John P. Koval. *Stress in the Ministry*. Washington, D.C.: Ministry Studies Board, 1971.

Nance, Terry. *God's Armor Bearer: How to Serve God's Leaders*. Tulsa, Okla.: Harrison House, 1990.

Nouwen, Henri J. M. *Out of Solitude: Three Meditations on the Christian Life*. Notre Dame, Ind.: Ave Maria Press, 1984.

Oswald, Roy M. *Clergy Self-Care: Finding a Balance for Effective Ministry*. Washington, D.C.: Alban Institute, 1991.

———. "Why Do Clergy Wives Burn Out?" *Action Information*, January-February 1984.

Rainer, Thom. *Effective Evangelistic Churches*. Nashville: Broadman & Holman, 1996.

Rubietta, Jane. *Quiet Places: A Woman's Guide to Personal Retreat*. Minneapolis: Bethany House, 1997.

Schafler, Dale. *Seven Promises of a Promise Keeper*. Colorado Springs, Colo.: Focus on the Family/Word, 1994.

Shelley, Marshall. *Healthy Hectic Home*. Waco, Tex.: Word, 1988.

Southern Baptist Convention Virginia Newspaper, December 1990.

Ulstein, Stefan. *Pastors Off the Record: Straight Talk About Life in the Ministry*. Downers Grove, Ill.: InterVarsity Press, 1993.

Willimon, William H. *Clergy and Laity Burnout*. Nashville: Abingdon, 1989.

Willis, Charles. "Lifeway Executive Addresses Churches' 'Dirty Little Secret.'" *BPNews*, May 5, 1999 <www.BPNews.net>.

Wingfield, Mark. "Clergy Want More Family Support." *The Standard*, June 16, 1999.

Zikmund, Barbara Brown, Adair T. Lummis and Patricia M. Y. Chang. *Clergy Women: An Uphill Calling*. Louisville, Ky.: Westminster John Knox, 1998.

Additional Resources

Clergy Appreciation Month Planning Guide. Colorado Springs, Colo.: Focus on the Family.

Epstein, J. David. *Clergy Tax 2001*. Ventura, Calif.: Regal, 2001.

Heim, Pamela Hoover. *The Pastor's Wife: Balancing Her Multiple Relationships*. Arlington Heights, Ill.: Harvest Publications, 2001.

Lee, Cameron. *PK: Helping Pastors' Kids Through Their Identity Crisis*. Grand Rapids, Mich.: Zondervan, 1992.

MacDonald, Gordon. *Mid-Course Correction: Re-ordering Your Private World for the Next Part of the Journey.* Nashville: Thomas Nelson, 2000.

Mains, Karen. *Comforting One Another.* Nashville: Thomas Nelson, 1997.

McBurney, Louis. *Every Pastor Needs a Pastor.* Marble, Colo.: Marble Retreat, 1977.

Melander, Rochelle, and Harold Eppley. *The Spiritual Leader's Guide to Self-Care.* Washington, D.C.: Alban Institute, 2002.

Pastoral Care Directory: Personal Resources for Ministers and their Families. Colorado Springs, Colo.: Focus on the Family.

Schaumburg, Harry W., M.D. *False Intimacy: Understanding the Struggle of Sexual Addiction.* Colorado Springs, Colo.: NavPress, 1997.

Contact Information

If your church, board, women's ministry or special events coordinator is interested in considering the author for a conference, retreat, banquet or training event, please contact:

Jane Rubietta
Abounding Ministries
225 Bluff Avenue
Grayslake, IL 60030
Jrubietta@abounding.org
www.abounding.org